Cooking Italian

ANTIPASTI

THUNDER BAY
P·R·E·S·S

Editorial Director: Cristina Cappa Legora
Editorial Coordinator: Valeria Camaschella
Translation: Studio Traduzioni Vecchia, Milan
North American Edition
Managing Editor: JoAnn Padgett
Associate Editor: Elizabeth McNulty

Table of Contents

First published in the United States by

Thunder Bay Press
5880 Oberlin Drive, Suite 400
San Diego, CA 92121-4794
1-800-284-3580
http://www.advmkt.com

Library of Congress Cataloging-in-Publication Data

Quaderni di cucina.   English.
    Cooking Italian.   Antipasti.
        p.   cm.
    Includes index.
    ISBN 1-57145-196-X
    1. Appetizers.   2. Cookery, Italian.   I. Title.
TX740.Q33 1999
641.8'12––dc21   99-25760
                                                     CIP

Printed in Singapore

1 2 3 4 5 99 00 01 02 03

Introduction

Cooking is a necessity and a pleasure. Or rather, necessity is transformed into pleasure. Today, we like to try out new ingredients whenever we can, inventing variations on traditional dishes, and experimenting with unusual types of cooking procedures.

This new series of books was designed to make cooking a pleasant pastime, with recipes based on our tradition that nevertheless often contain a little something extra, a flash of imagination, an exotic variation that makes the dish more appetizing and impressive.

The books you'll peruse will include a number of tools to help you achieve the best possible results without making mistakes or wasting time. First of all, look at the summary in each section, which will give you an immediate overview of the dishes included. The color illustrations will help you quickly choose the recipe you like best.

The recipes themselves are designed to be as practical as possible. The ingredients are clearly listed to the side, followed by the equipment necessary and a practical chart that summarizes everything you need to know right away, before you begin cooking: the degree of difficulty, preparation and cooking time, cooking method, how long the dish will keep, and so on. The description of the recipes is also extremely clear and detailed, and is divided into sections that cover each separate stage of the recipe.

Another important feature is the suggestion of an appropriate wine to be served with the dish. (These are just suggestions because we all know that wines are a matter of personal taste.) To make it easier for you, we have always selected wines with appellation contrôlée, with the official caption. Of course, we also provide the best temperature for serving each individual wine.

In addition, there are always practical, useful suggestions on the recipe itself (for example, whether you can change any ingredients, how to multiply a given dish), or related to preparation (for example, how to prevent ravioli from breaking as they cook).

Finally, we include a "special note" for each preparation—some extra information on an ingredient in the recipe that may be historical, scientific, dietetic and so forth—that further enriches the descriptions.

This book is devoted to ANTIPASTI, the royalty of Italian appetizers, and is full of tasty recipes, from the most simple to the most elegant. The recipes have been divided by seasonal appeal: spring and summer antipasti, fall and winter antipasti, and all-season antipasti, to make it easier to choose the right recipe for you.

Recipe Index

Tomatoes with Yogurt Stuffing p32

Fried Green Tomatoes p33

Raw Pickled Vegetables p34

Escarole and Pepper Salad p36

Stuffed Bell Pepper p38

Savory Watercress Tart p40

Bell Pepper Involtini with Tuna p42

Beef Carpaccio p44

Smoked Ham Drops p45

Spring and Summer Antipasti

Shallots alla Escoffier

INGREDIENTS

serves 4

I lb. — 500 g SHALLOTS
3 tablespoons EXTRA VIRGIN OLIVE OIL
I tablespoon SUGAR
1.5 oz. — 30 g SULTANA RAISINS
I sprig THYME
I BAY leaf
I teaspoon TOMATO PASTE
I teaspoon CORIANDER SEEDS
SALT and PEPPER to taste
1/2 teaspoon PAPRIKA
I cup DRY WHITE WINE
1/2 teaspoon VEGETABLE EXTRACT

EQUIPMENT

a saucepan

Difficulty	AVERAGE
Preparation Time	10 MIN.
Cooking Time	35 MIN.
Method of cooking	STOVETOP
Microwave	YES
Freezing	NO
Keeping Time	3 DAYS

SPECIAL NOTE

Auguste Escoffier (1846–1945), a French gourmet, became a chef *gardemanger* at the age of 23. His meeting with César Ritz at the Savoy of London marked the beginning of his world fame.

1 Clean the shallots and remove the roots, outer skin and the harder green portion. Wash and dry them with a kitchen towel. Place them in a saucepan, drizzle with olive oil, place them over moderate heat and cook, stirring gently with a wooden spoon. Sauté lightly for 2–3 minutes, then add the sugar and sultana raisins. Mix and add the washed and dried thyme and bay leaf.

2 Dissolve the tomato paste in a small amount of lukewarm water and add it to the shallots. Add the coriander seeds and season with a pinch of salt and freshly ground pepper.

3 Finally, sprinkle with paprika and toast it briefly. Bathe with white wine, then add 1/2 cup water and the vegetable extract.

4 Mix, cover the saucepan and cook the shallots over moderate heat for about 25 minutes, stirring occasionally. When done, remove from the heat and serve lukewarm in the pan.

PRACTICAL SUGGESTIONS
When well washed and finely chopped, the green parts of shallots can be used to flavor a mixed vegetable salad or to add fragrance to an omelet.

Tuna, Bean and Olive Salad

RECOMMENDED WINES

Riviera Ligure di Ponente Pigato: dry white wine served at 50°F / 10 °C

Trebbiano di Romagna: dry white wine served at 50°F / 10 °C

1 Place the beans in a mixing bowl with a large amount of cold water and soak for about 6 hours. Trim the carrot, peel it with a potato peeler and wash it. Clean the celery, wash it and remove the threads. Trim the arugula, wash it and dry gently with a dishcloth.

2 Drain the beans, rinse and place in a saucepan with the celery, carrot and bay leaf. Cover with water and add a pinch of salt, then slowly bring to a boil and cook about an hour.

3 Drain the beans, removing the vegetables, cool them and place in a salad bowl. Add the crumbled tuna, the peeled and finely sliced scallion and the pitted green olives.

4 Beat the oil, vinegar, salt, freshly ground pepper and minced parsley in a bowl and blend well. Pour the dressing on the prepared salad, mix and serve, garnishing with little garden arugula leaves.

PRACTICAL SUGGESTIONS

This cool, delicious salad could be an excellent second course, if you increase the ingredients slightly. If you're in a hurry, you can use canned beans instead of dry.

INGREDIENTS

serves 4

1/4 lb. – 100 g DRY WHITE BEANS

1 CARROT

1/2 stalk CELERY

2 oz. – 1 bunch ARUGULA (GARDEN ROCKET)

1 BAY leaf

SALT and PEPPER to taste

4 oz. – 100 g TUNA PACKED IN OIL

1 SCALLION

scant 4 oz. – 80 g MILD GREEN OLIVES

4 tablespoons EXTRA VIRGIN OLIVE OIL

2 tablespoons WHITE WINE VINEGAR

2 oz. – 1 bunch PARSLEY

EQUIPMENT

1 pot

1 frying pan

1 large, tall skillet

Difficulty	**AVERAGE**
Preparation Time	**15 MIN. + 6 HOURS**
Cooking Time	**1 HOUR**
Method of cooking	**STOVETOP**
Microwave	**NO**
Freezing	**NO**
Keeping Time	**1 DAY**

SPECIAL NOTE

Arugula has been used as a medicinal herb in southern Europe since Roman times. Today it is popular primarily in France, Italy and Egypt.

Vol–au–Vents with String Bean Cream

INGREDIENTS

serves 4

3/4 lb. – 300 g STRING BEANS
2 cups FRESH CREAM
1/4 cup – 40 g BUTTER
I EGG YOLK
4 tablespoons GRATED PARMESAN CHEESE
SALT and PEPPER to taste
8–I0 FROZEN VOL–AU–VENTS

EQUIPMENT

a pot
a blender
a saucepan
a serving dish

Difficulty	EASY
Preparation Time	I5 MIN.
Cooking Time	20 MIN.
Method of cooking	STOVETOP AND OVEN
Microwave	YES
Freezing	NO
Keeping Time	2 DAYS

SPECIAL NOTE

Vol-au-vents are made of an especially light dough (hence its name in French: "flight on the wind"), and were invented in the 18th century by A. Carême.

Recommended Wines
Prosecco di Conegliano (Veneto):
mellow, aromatic white wine served at 50°F / 10°C
Colli di Luni bianco (Liguria): dry white wine served at 50°F / 10°C

❖

I Wash the string beans and remove the outer threads. Bring a generous amount of lightly salted water to boil in a large pot. Add the string beans and boil for about 15 minutes. Drain and place in the blender with the cream, then blend until you obtain a uniform mixture.

2 Melt the butter in a saucepan, add the blended beans and cream the egg yolk and the parmesan, and mix with a wooden spoon until the ingredients are well blended. Let it season for 5 minutes, then add salt and pepper.

3 Heat the vol-au-vents in the oven, fill with the prepared mixture place on a serving dish, and decorate them as you like.

Practical Suggestions
This recipe is delicious with the string beans as indicated, but it is equally good if you use other vegetables, for example strips of green pepper sautéed with a bit of oil and whipped, or boiled carrots and Swiss chard.

Vegetable Medley

INGREDIENTS

serves 4

1/4 lb. – 100 g SHELLED PEAS
1/4 lb. – 100 g SHELLED LIMA BEANS
1/4 lb. – 100 g TURNIPS
1/4 lb. – 100 g CARROTS
1/4 lb. – 100 g STRING BEANS
1/2 CAULIFLOWER
2 tablespoons BALSAMIC VINEGAR
SALT and PEPPER to taste
2 tablespoons EXTRA VIRGIN OLIVE OIL
1/4 lb. – 100 g HAM, in one piece
1/4 lb. – 100 g CUCUMBERS
1 tablespoon MAYONNAISE
1 tablespoon CAPERS

EQUIPMENT

a pot, a frying pan
a small bowl, 5 bowls
a skillet, a salad bowl

Difficulty	AVERAGE
Preparation Time	30 MIN. + 15 MIN.
Cooking Time	50 MIN.
Method of cooking	STOVETOP
Microwave	NO
Freezing	NO
Keeping Time	1 DAY

SPECIAL NOTE

In some regions in Italy (such as Friuli–Venezia Giulia), turnips are preserved in vinegar using a method similar to that for sauerkraut. The resulting preparation is called *brovada*.

Recommended Wines
Biferno bianco (Molise): dry white wine served at 50°F / 10°C
Cirò bianco (Calabria): dry white wine served at 50°F / 10°C

❖

1 Wash the peas and beans, trim the turnips and carrots, and peel, wash and chop separately into strips. Trim the string beans, remove any threads, wash and chop them into pieces. Clean the cauliflower, divide into florets and wash.

2 Boil all the vegetables separately in a skillet of boiling, salted water: the beans for 20 minutes, the peas and cauliflower florets for 10 minutes, and the strips of carrot and turnip for about 5–7 minutes. Drain, run immediately under cold water, dry and place in separate bowls.

3 In the meantime, place the salt, freshly ground pepper and balsamic vinegar in a small bowl and mix until the salt is completely dissolved. Add the oil and mix lightly with a fork until the sauce is well emulsified. Pour a little into each bowl of vegetables and marinate about 15 minutes.

4 In the meantime, cut the ham and cucumbers into strips, place them in the middle of a salad bowl and arrange the prepared vegetables around them. Add the mayonnaise and capers and serve.

Practical Suggestions
If you're in a hurry, you can prepare this "salad" with frozen vegetables. If you want to give it a more pronounced flavor, use mustard instead of mayonnaise.

Frittata delle Langhe

INGREDIENTS

serves 4

4 oz. – 100 g SMALL DARK GREEN
LETTUCE LEAVES
2 oz. – 1 bunch AROMATIC HERBS
1/2 clove GARLIC
6 EGGS
3 tablespoons GRATED PARMESAN CHEESE
1 pinch NUTMEG
SALT and PEPPER to taste
4 tablespoons EXTRA VIRGIN OLIVE OIL
1 ROBIOLA CHEESE
or other soft, fresh cheese
6 oz.– 150 g TUNA CANNED IN OIL

EQUIPMENT

2 mixing bowls
a frying pan
aluminum foil
a serving dish

Difficulty	AVERAGE
Preparation Time	30 MIN. + 12 HOURS
Cooking Time	10 MIN.
Method of cooking	STOVETOP
Microwave	NO
Freezing	NO
Keeping Time	2 DAYS

SPECIAL NOTE

Garlic has been known since ancient times. It was
a common food for the Romans until the first
century, when it began to lose popularity because
of its bad odor, as noted by Varro and Horace.

RECOMMENDED WINES
*Cortese dell'Alto Monferrato (Piedmont):
mellow, aromatic white wine served at 50°F / 10°C
White Pisano di S. Torpé (Tuscany): dry white wine served at 50°F / 10°C*

1 Trim and wash the lettuce, drain and mince. Wash the bunch of
aromatic herbs, dry them and mince them, then place them in a small
bowl. Peel the garlic and mince.

2 Break the eggs into a mixing bowl, beat, add the minced lettuce,
the grated parmesan, part of the minced aromatic herbs, the minced
garlic, the nutmeg, the salt and freshly ground pepper and mix all
ingredients well.

3 Add 3 tablespoons olive oil to a frying pan, add the prepared
mixture and cook the omelet. Turn it onto a plate, and using a knife
square the edges.

4 Using a fork, crush the robiola in another mixing bowl, add the
crumbled tuna, a teaspoon of oil and the remaining minced aromatic
herbs. Mix the various ingredients until you obtain a creamy, thick
mixture. Spread this on the square omelet, roll it up and wrap it in a
sheet of aluminum foil. Cool it in the refrigerator for 12 hours.
When serving, remove the aluminum foil, cut the roll into slices,
place on a serving dish and serve.

PRACTICAL SUGGESTIONS

*You can use spinach in this tasty omelet instead of the lettuce. If you want
to make it more substantial and serve it as a main course, you can use 6 oz.
– 150 g finely chopped ham instead of the tuna.*

Mimosa Crostini with Asparagus

INGREDIENTS

serves 4

2 EGGS
1 sprig PARSLEY
SALT and PEPPER to taste
4 square slices OF BREAD
16 boiled ASPARAGUS TIPS
1/8 cup — 20 g BUTTER

EQUIPMENT

a vegetable mill
a baking dish
a small saucepan

Difficulty	EASY
Preparation Time	15 MIN.
Cooking Time	15 MIN.
Method of cooking	OVEN
Microwave	YES
Freezing	NO
Keeping Time	1 DAY

SPECIAL NOTE

The part of the asparagus plant that we eat is the turions, the cylindrical buds produced by the rhizomes, gathered before they become leaves. They can be green, white, or, more rarely, pink.

RECOMMENDED WINES
Colli Piacentini Val Nure (Emilia Romagna):
dry white wine served at 50°F / 10°C
Cortese di Gavi (Piedmont):
mellow, aromatic white wine served at 50°F / 10°C

1 Boil a generous quantity of salted water in a pot, then add the eggs and let them cook 8–10 minutes. Drain, run under cold water to stop the cooking process, and peel. Run them through a vegetable mill (using the medium-sized holes), and place the mixture in a bowl. Preheat the oven to 350°F.

2 Trim, wash and thoroughly dry the parsley, mince it finely and add it to the eggs. Season with a pinch of salt and freshly ground pepper and blend the ingredients well with a wooden spoon.

3 Butter the slices of bread and cut in half to make 8 rectangles. On each rectangle, first place a thin layer of minced hardboiled egg and then 2 asparagus tips. Place these crostini in a buttered baking dish and bake for 5 minutes. Remove and serve hot.

PRACTICAL SUGGESTIONS
When not in season, you can still get excellent results by using frozen asparagus tips instead of fresh. You can also sprinkle the crostini with a pinch of dill, chervil and tarragon.

Chicken Salad Primavera

INGREDIENTS

serves 4

1 CARROT

1 stalk CELERY

1 ONION

1 lb. – 400 g CHICKEN BREAST

3/4 lb. – 300 g STRING BEANS

6 oz. – 150 g SHELLED PEAS

2 tablespoons WHITE WINE VINEGAR

SALT to taste

1 teaspoon MUSTARD

4 tablespoons EXTRA VIRGIN OLIVE OIL

EQUIPMENT

a skillet

a mixing bowl

a small bowl

pot for steam cooking

Difficulty	AVERAGE
Preparation Time	20 MIN.
Cooking Time	50 MIN.
Method of cooking	STOVETOP
Microwave	NO
Freezing	YES
Keeping Time	1 DAY

SPECIAL NOTE

Chicken breast was always highly prized, as can be seen from the French name for chicken fillets, *suprêmes*, which in fact means "supreme."

RECOMMENDED WINES

Oltrepò Pavese rosso (Lombardy): light red wine served at 57°F / 14°C

Bianco Vergine Valdichiana (Tuscany): dry white wine served at 50°F / 10°C

1 Peel the carrot, clean the celery and peel the onion (setting half of it aside). Wash them and place them in a large skillet with about 2 cups – 1/2 liter water. Heat and bring to a boil, lower the heat and boil for 15 minutes. Salt, then add the chicken breast and continue cooking for another 15 minutes without boiling.

2 In the meantime, trim the string beans and wash them. Wash the peas, place them in the steamer with the string beans and steam about 10–12 minutes.

3 Drain the chicken breast, cool and dice. Place it in a mixing bowl and add the boiled peas and string beans.

4 Finely mince the remaining onion, place it in a small bowl, add the vinegar mixed with a pinch of salt, then add the mustard and oil. Lightly beat the ingredients with a fork until the sauce is well emulsified. Season the chicken salad and vegetables with the dressing, mix and serve immediately.

PRACTICAL SUGGESTIONS

If you increase the ingredients a bit, this rich, nutritious appetizer could be an unusual entrée for a summer lunch. It is also an excellent way to use leftover chicken.

Tricolor Eggs

INGREDIENTS
serves 4

4 EGGS
1 tablespoon WHITE WINE VINEGAR
SALT to taste
1 handful BOILED SPINACH
2 tablespoons TOMATO SAUCE

For the mayonnaise
1 EGG YOLK
SALT to taste
OLIVE OIL to taste
1 LEMON

EQUIPMENT
1 small saucepan
1 slotted spoon, a mixing bowl
a pastry syringe
a fluted tip
3 bowls, a serving dish

Difficulty	AVERAGE
Preparation Time	30 MIN.
Cooking Time	20 MIN.
Method of cooking	STOVETOP
Microwave	NO
Freezing	NO
Keeping Time	1 DAY

SPECIAL NOTE
Eggs are rich in protein and energy—providing substances (iron, vitamin A, lecithin and neutral fats). This high nutritive content makes eggs a valuable food for children and the elderly.

RECOMMENDED WINES
Breganze bianco (Veneto): dry white wine served at 50°F / 10°C
Colli Piacentini Ortrugo (Emilia Romagna):
dry white wine served at 50°F / 10°C

1 Prepare the eggs: boil water in a small saucepan to which you have added a tablespoon of vinegar and two pinches salt. Break an egg in a plate and let it slide into the boiling water. Cook for 4–5 minutes, then remove with a slotted spoon. Repeat for each egg.

2 Carefully clean the spinach. Wash it repeatedly under running water, drain it well, and using a chopping knife, mince very finely then set aside.

3 Prepare the mayonnaise: place the egg yolk in a mixing bowl with a pinch of salt, beat it with a wooden spoon until it begins to grow somewhat thick, then add the oil drop by drop, stirring continuously. When the sauce has become quite thick and dense add the lemon juice, stirring constantly.

4 Divide the mayonnaise into 3 bowls. Leave one portion as it is, blend the tomato sauce with the next portion, and blend the minced spinach to the last portion. Place the eggs on a serving dish and using a pastry syringe, decorate with the tricolor mayonnaise.

PRACTICAL SUGGESTIONS
For best results when making mayonnaise, the eggs must be very fresh, and all ingredients must be kept at room temperature for at least 3 hours before you use them. If the sauce separates, put an egg yolk into another bowl and stirring constantly, slowly add the separated mayonnaise to it.

Poached Eggs with Tomatoes

RECOMMENDED WINES
Oltrepò Pavese Pinot bianco (Lombardy):
dry white wine served at 50°F / 10°C
Castel del Monte rosato (Puglia): rosé served at 50°F / 10°C

❖

1 Place about a half a quart – 1 liter water in a skillet with the coarse salt and a tablespoon of vinegar. Place on the heat and bring to a boil. In the meantime, break the eggs into a plate and when the water comes to a boil, slide them in (if they don't all fit, do this in two separate operations).

2 Boil for 3 minutes, or better yet, until the egg white has hardened enough to cover the yolk. Using a slotted spoon, remove the eggs and drain them on a dishtowel. Using a very sharp knife, trim the edges of the whites, then place them on a serving dish.

3 Wash the tomatoes and chop some of them into slices and some into cubes. Arrange these harmoniously on the plate around the eggs. Season with a pinch of salt, vinegar and oil. Garnish with the chopped anchovies and washed, chopped basil, then serve.

INGREDIENTS

serves 6

1 tablespoon COARSE SALT
2 tablespoons APPLE CIDER VINEGAR
6 EGGS
2 lb. – 900 g TOMATOES
6 pinches FINE SALT
4 tablespoons EXTRA VIRGIN OLIVE OIL
6 ANCHOVIES IN OIL
1 sprig BASIL

EQUIPMENT

a skillet
a slotted spoon
a serving dish

Difficulty	**EASY**
Preparation Time	**15 MIN.**
Cooking Time	**3 MIN. – 6 MIN.**
Method of cooking	**STOVETOP**
Microwave	**NO**
Freezing	**NO**
Keeping Time	**1 DAY**

PRACTICAL SUGGESTIONS
To prevent poached eggs from shriveling as they cool, immerse them in cold water as soon as they are drained. When you want to serve them hot, you can also prepare them in advance. To reheat, just immerse them once again in hot but not boiling water for a few seconds.

SPECIAL NOTE
Salt is the common name for the type of sodium chloride used for food purposes. In nature, it is found in sea water and some springs, and appears in the crystalline state as rock salt.

Decorated Hardboiled Eggs

INGREDIENTS

serves 4

1/8 cup — 30 g BUTTER
8 EGGS
2–3 tablespoons ANCHOVY PASTE
1 teaspoon MAYONNAISE
PEPPER to taste
8 CAPERS
RADISHES to taste
CUCUMBERS to taste

EQUIPMENT

a bowl
a small saucepan
a pastry syringe
a serving dish

Difficulty	AVERAGE
Preparation Time	30 MIN.
Cooking Time	10 MIN.
Method of cooking	STOVETOP
Microwave	NO
Freezing	NO
Keeping Time	1 DAY

SPECIAL NOTE

Cucumber juice is helpful for alleviating irritation and redness of the skin. It's also a fine remedy for cracked, rough hands, as well as an excellent astringent.

RECOMMENDED WINES

Orvieto classico (Umbria): mellow, aromatic white wine served at 50°F / 10°C
Franciacorta bianco (Lombardy): dry white wine served at 50°F / 10°C

1 Take the butter from the refrigerator at least 30 minutes before using it, so it will soften, and put it in a bowl. Hardboil the eggs in a pan of boiling water for 10 minutes, then run them under cold water and dry.

2 With a small, sharp knife, cut the white in a zigzag pattern about two thirds up the egg, being careful not to cut the yolk. When you've cut it all the way around, remove the white cap. Repeat for all the eggs.

3 Add the anchovy paste, mayonnaise and a pinch of freshly ground pepper to the bowl of butter, and beat everything together until the mixture becomes foamy. Put it in a pastry syringe and squirt a little on each egg, decorating the top. End with a caper in the center.

4 Place the eggs on a serving dish on which you have arranged a few leaves of fresh lettuce and decorate with radishes and cucumbers cut into slices. Serve the eggs after refrigerating them for at least 10 minutes to allow the butter mixture to harden a bit.

PRACTICAL SUGGESTIONS

If you're not fond of anchovy paste, you can obtain excellent results with 4 oz. — 100 g salted anchovies instead. Wash them, remove the bones and the head, and put through the blender.

Garden Salad

INGREDIENTS

serves 4

4 POTATOES

4 ZUCCHINI

1/2 lb. – 200 g STRING BEANS

1 bunch ARUGULA (GARDEN ROCKET)

1 bunch RADICCHIO

2 TOMATOES

1 CUCUMBER

1 HARDBOILED EGG

1 teaspoon MUSTARD

4 tablespoons OLIVE OIL

juice of one LEMON

SALT and PEPPER to taste

EQUIPMENT

a pot

a bowl

a serving dish

Difficulty	AVERAGE
Preparation Time	30 MIN.
Cooking Time	40 MIN.
Method of cooking	STOVETOP
Microwave	YES
Freezing	NO
Keeping Time	1 DAY

SPECIAL NOTE

Chioggia and Verona radicchio are usually used for salads, while Castelfranco and Treviso radicchio are better for risotto and grilled dishes.

RECOMMENDED WINES

Cortese di Gavi (Piedmont):

mellow, aromatic white wine served at 50°F / 10°C

Locorotondo bianco (Puglia): dry white wine served at 50°F / 10°C

1 Peel and wash the potatoes, trim and wash the zucchini, trim the string beans and remove any threads. Boil these vegetables separately in a large pot of salted water, then drain and cool.

2 In the meantime, clean the arugula and radicchio, wash the leaves, dry them and cut into thin strips. Then slice the zucchini, potatoes, tomatoes and cucumber.

3 Mince the hardboiled egg, place it in a bowl and add the mustard, oil, lemon juice, a pinch of salt and freshly ground pepper, mix and beat the mixture with a fork. You should obtain a rather thin sauce.

4 Arrange the potatoes in the middle of a round serving dish, then arrange the zucchini around them, then the string beans, being careful to place them around in a ring. Arrange the slices of tomato around the string beans, and then place the mixed arugula and radicchio on the edge of the plate. Drizzle uniformly with the sauce and serve: your salad will look like a fresh, flowering garden.

PRACTICAL SUGGESTIONS

To make the cucumber more digestible, you should peel it, cut it into slices, put it on a plate, sprinkle it slightly with a pinch of salt and let it sit for at least a half hour. Then pour off the vegetable liquid that has formed.

Trout and Surimi Mousse

INGREDIENTS

serves 8–10

1 1/2 lb. – 600 g TROUT FILLETS
5 tablespoons – 50 g CREAM
3 EGGS
2 tablespoons EXTRA VIRGIN OLIVE OIL
1 teaspoon MUSTARD
SALT to taste
1/2 lb. – 200 g SHELLED PEAS
4/5 lb. – 350 g SURIMI
juice of one LEMON

EQUIPMENT

a mixing bowl, a bowl
a skillet
a rectangular mold
a double boiler
aluminum foil
a serving dish

Difficulty	**AVERAGE**
Preparation Time	**30 MIN. + 7 HOURS**
Cooking Time	**35 MIN.**
Method of cooking	**STOVETOP**
Microwave	**NO**
Freezing	**NO**
Keeping Time	**2 DAYS**

SPECIAL NOTE

Surimi sticks, or imitation crab legs, are prepared with crab meat. Sometimes you can find less expensive ones with a mixture of crab and cod.

Valcalepio bianco (Lombardy): dry white wine served at 50°F / 10°C
Etna bianco (Sicily): dry white wine served at 50°F / 10°C

1 Finely mince the trout fillets, place them in a mixing bowl, add the cream, and then add the egg yolks one at a time. Mix and add a bit of oil. In a bowl, whip the cream to stiff peaks and gently fold into the mixture. Add the mustard, a pinch of salt, mix to blend, and place the mousse in the refrigerator.

2 Cook the peas in a skillet of salted, boiling water, then drain and cool. Place the surimi sticks on a plate, drizzle with lemon juice and sprinkle with a pinch of salt. Preheat the oven to 400°F.

3 Line the mold with a sheet of aluminum foil, spread a layer of trout mousse on the bottom, add some of the peas on top, then another layer of mousse. Place the surimi sticks side by side and continue, repeating the layers until the ingredients are finished. Be sure to end with the surimi sticks.

4 Put the bowl over a double boiler in a hot oven for about 20 minutes. Remove, cool to room temperature and refrigerate for at least 6 hours. To serve, turn out the trout and surimi mousse, place it on a serving dish and slice.

PRACTICAL SUGGESTIONS

Before turning over the mousse, immerse the mold in hot water for a few moments, which will prevent it from sticking to the mold. If you like, you can use frozen fillets of trout.

Rainbow Tart

INGREDIENTS

serves 4

For the dough

2 cups – 250 g WHITE FLOUR

1/2 cup – 125 g BUTTER

SALT to taste

For the filling

1 lb. – 400 g ZUCCHINI

1/4 cup – 50 g BUTTER

SALT and PEPPER to taste

1 lb. – 400 g CARROTS, boiled al dente

1/2 lb. – 250 g FROZEN PEAS

5 EGGS

2 tablespoons CREAM

pinch of THYME

pinch of MARJORAM

2 oz. – 50 g GRATED GRUYÈRE CHEESE

EQUIPMENT

2 frying pans, a small frying pan, a round pie pan a mixing bowl, aluminum foil, dry beans

Difficulty	**AVERAGE**
Preparation Time	**30 MIN. + 30 MIN.**
Cooking Time	**1 HOUR + 30 MIN.**
Method of cooking	**STOVETOP AND OVEN**
Microwave	**YES**
Freezing	**YES**
Keeping Time	**2 DAYS**

SPECIAL NOTE

Marjoram was introduced to Europe in the Middle Ages. Ladies prized it for bouquets of flowers, perfumed bags and scented bath water.

RECOMMENDED WINES
Piave Tokay italico (Veneto):
mellow, aromatic white wine served at 50°F / 10°C
Cirò bianco (Calabria): dry white wine served at 50°F / 10°C

❖

1 Quickly blend the flour with the butter, salt and a few teaspoon ice water. Place the dough in a sheet of aluminum foil and refrigerat 30 minutes.

2 Wash and trim the zucchini, cut into rounds, sauté for a few minutes in a pan with a scant 1/8 cup – 20 grams butter, and season with salt and pepper. Peel and chop the carrots into rounds, then season over the heat with a scant 1/8 cup – 20 grams butter, in another frying pan. Now melt 1/2 oz. – 10 grams butter in a small frying pan, add the peas and cook, gradually adding water. Season with salt and pepper. Preheat the oven to 350°F.

3 Roll the dough out on a lightly floured cutting board and fit it to a round pie pan. Poke a few holes in it with a fork, place the beans on it, and bake for 20 minutes. Remove from the oven, remove the bean and place the zucchini rounds on it in concentric circles. Make another circle with the carrot rounds, and end with the peas Continue this way, alternating the various vegetables. Beat the eggs in a bowl with salt and pepper, add the cream, thyme, marjoram and gruyère, blend and pour over the vegetables. Bake about 40 minute and serve either hot or cold.

PRACTICAL SUGGESTIONS

If you want to prepare this faster, you can use phyllo dough or frozen pât brisée instead of making the pie dough. You can also prepare the tart th day before and serve it cold or reheated in the oven.

Tomato Baskets

INGREDIENTS
serves 4

1/2 lb. – 200 g STALE HOMEMADE
BREAD CRUMBS
4 SALTED ANCHOVIES
1 clove GARLIC
1 sprig PARSLEY
6 tablespoons EXTRA VIRGIN OLIVE OIL
SALT to taste
4 TOMATOES

EQUIPMENT
a small saucepan
a baking sheet
a serving dish

Difficulty	AVERAGE
Preparation Time	15 MIN.
Cooking Time	25 MIN.
Method of cooking	STOVETOP AND OVEN
Microwave	YES
Freezing	NO
Keeping Time	1 DAY

SPECIAL NOTE
The nutritional value of bread depends primarily
on its carbohydrates. Every 4 oz. – 100 g of
yeast bread contains more than 2 oz. – 62
grams of carbohydrates, although there is
somewhat less in rye bread.

RECOMMENDED WINES
Biferno bianco (Molise): dry white wine served at 50°F / 10°C
Colli Piacentini Monterosso Val d'Arda (Lombardy):
dry white wine served at 50°F / 10°C

1 Cut the bread into cubes about 1/2 inch – 1 centimeter square.
Remove the salt from the anchovies, remove the head and backbone,
and break them up coarsely. Peel the garlic and mince it with the
washed, trimmed parsley.

2 Place all these ingredients in a small saucepan with 4 tablespoons
oil. Place over low heat and toast the bread, stirring with a wooden
spoon, being sure to season everything and blend all the flavors.
Finally, if it seems necessary, season with a pinch of salt. Preheat the
oven to 400°F.

3 Wash the tomatoes, dry them, cut them in half horizontally and
hollow them out with a sharp knife, removing most of the pulp, then
fill them with the toasted bread and its seasoning.

4 Place the tomato baskets on baking sheet greased with the
remaining oil, and bake for about 20 minutes. Remove from the
oven, transfer to a serving dish and serve hot.

PRACTICAL SUGGESTIONS
The cubes of bread described in this recipe can also be a tasty seasoning for
a plate of pasta, preferably the short variety. Just add a bit of olive oil at
the last minute (to prevent the bread from becoming soggy).

Tomatoes with Yogurt Stuffing

INGREDIENTS

serves 4

4 TOMATOES

2 tablespoons NATURAL YOGURT

I container LOW-FAT COTTAGE CHEESE

YOLK OF one HARDBOILED EGG

I small SCALLION, finely minced

SALT and PEPPER to taste

6 MINT leaves

I sprig CHIVES

3 tablespoons unsweetened WHIPPED CREAM

To garnish

4 rings HOT GREEN PEPPER

cut from two peppers

4 small BLACK GREEK OLIVES

EQUIPMENT

a mixer, a mixing bowl

a pastry bag with a fluted tip

absorbent paper towels, 4 small single plates

Difficulty	**AVERAGE**
Preparation Time	**20 MIN. + 30 MIN.**
Cooking Time	**NO**
Method of cooking	**NO**
Microwave	**NO**
Freezing	**NO**
Keeping Time	**I DAY**

SPECIAL NOTE

Mint leaves can be gathered for cooking any time
of the year. Remember that the more tender
leaves have a sweeter, more delicate flavor than
older leaves.

RECOMMENDED WINES
Frascati (Lazio): dry white wine served at 50°F / 10°C
Prosecco di Conegliano (Veneto):
mellow, aromatic white wine served at 50°F / 10°C

❖

I Wash and dry the tomatoes, cut the crown and remove the seed
and part of the pulp. Sprinkle with a bit of salt and arrange with th
open part down on a tilted cutting board. Let them sit for about 3
minutes until they lose their vegetable water.

2 In the meantime, use the mixer to blend the yogurt with th
cottage cheese, the hardboiled egg yolk and the minced scallion
until you have a uniform, pasty mixture. Place it in a mixing bow
and season it with a pinch of salt and freshly ground white pepper
Finally, add the finely minced mint, the chives and the whippe
cream. Mix again gently with a wooden spoon to blend th
ingredients well.

3 Take the hollow tomatoes, squeeze them gently and dry th
inside with absorbent paper towels.

4 Put the mixture into a pastry bag with a fluted tip, fill th
tomatoes and place them in the refrigerator. Before serving, plac
them on small single plates, decorating the top of each with a ring o
pepper. Place a black olive in the center.

PRACTICAL SUGGESTIONS

*These stuffed tomatoes are also good in place of a first course for a summe
luncheon; just double the ingredients. If you want them to be even lighter
use nonfat yogurt.*

Fried Green Tomatoes

RECOMMENDED WINES
Erbaluce di Caluso (Piedmont): dry white wine served at 50°F / 10°C
Vernaccia di San Gimignano (Tuscany):
mellow, aromatic white wine served at 50°F / 10°C

1 Clean and wash the tomatoes, chop horizontally into rather thick slices, salt and let them sit in a bowl for about 30 minutes, to eliminate the vegetable water.

2 Drain the tomatoes, dry them with absorbent paper towels and dip them first in the flour, then in the beaten egg, and finally in the bread crumbs.

3 Heat the oil in a frying pan. When the temperature is right, add the sliced tomato and sauté for a few minutes on each side, then place them on a sheet of absorbent paper towels to absorb any excess grease. Place them on a serving dish, garnish with a few sprigs of lettuce and slices of lemon, and serve hot.

INGREDIENTS
serves 4

4 GREEN TOMATOES
SALT to taste
WHITE FLOUR as necessary
I EGG
BREAD CRUMBS as necessary
SESAME OIL for frying
or peanut oil

EQUIPMENT
a mixing bowl
a frying pan
absorbent paper towels
a serving dish

Difficulty	**EASY**
Preparation Time	**I5 MIN.**
Cooking Time	**I5 MIN.**
Method of cooking	**STOVETOP**
Microwave	**NO**
Freezing	**NO**
Keeping Time	**2 DAYS**

PRACTICAL SUGGESTIONS
Green tomatoes breaded in this manner will be an original alternative to classic appetizers with fried vegetables. You can also serve them with breaded macaroons and apple rounds fried in batter.

SPECIAL NOTE
Considered an insignificant or even poisonous fruit until the 18th century, the tomato later became an essential part of cooking, particularly in Mediterranean cuisine.

Raw Pickled Vegetables

INGREDIENTS

serves 4

3 1/2–4 1/2 lb. – 1.5–2 kg RAW VEGETABLES
OF YOUR CHOICE
1/2–2/3 lb. each type
COARSE SALT as necessary
1/2 quart – 1 liter APPLE CIDER VINEGAR
half a clove of GARLIC per jar
BASIL as necessary
EXTRA VIRGIN OLIVE OIL as necessary

EQUIPMENT

salad bowl
glass jars with hermetic seals

Difficulty	**EASY**
Preparation Time	**30 MIN. + 28 HOURS**
Cooking Time	**NO**
Method of cooking	**NO**
Microwave	**NO**
Freezing	**NO**
Keeping Time	**3 MONTHS**

SPECIAL NOTE

The Italian name for this appetizer, *giardinera*,
comes from the French *jardinier*, which means
gardener, a reference to the fact that a gardener
has many kinds of fresh vegetables available.

RECOMMENDED WINES
Torgiano bianco (Umbria): dry white wine served at 50°F / 10°C
Colli di Luni bianco (Liguria): dry white wine served at 50°F / 10°C

1 Clean, carefully wash and chop the seasonal vegetables of you
choice for this recipe. Place them in a salad bowl and add a handful o
coarse salt for every 2.2 pounds – 1 kilo of vegetables.

2 Let it sit for 24 hours, then drain the vegetables and return them
to the salad bowl. Cover them with apple cider vinegar and let them
sit another 4 hours.

3 Drain the vegetables well and place them in a glass jar or bottle
with the peeled garlic and washed and dried basil (if necessary, use
more than one jar). Finally, cover with olive oil and seal the jar well

PRACTICAL SUGGESTIONS
*You can use any kind of vegetable for this recipe, as long as it has a firm
flesh. When stored in a cool, dry, dark place, the vegetables will keep
perfectly for several months. Once open, however, the jar should be kept in
the refrigerator and the vegetables should be consumed within a short time.*

Escarole and Pepper Salad

INGREDIENTS

serves 4

1 head of ESCAROLE
1 YELLOW PEPPER
1/2 lb. – 200 g FRESH MOZZARELLA
1 tablespoon LEMON JUICE
3 tablespoons EXTRA VIRGIN OLIVE OIL
SALT and PEPPER to taste

EQUIPMENT

a salad bowl

Difficulty	EASY
Preparation Time	15 MIN.
Cooking Time	NO
Method of cooking	NO
Microwave	NO
Freezing	NO
Keeping Time	1 DAY

SPECIAL NOTE

Escarole, from the Italian term, *scarola*, comes from the Latin *escarius*, or "edible." It is a variety of endive with rather large, not very curly leaves, with white inner leaves.

RECOMMENDED WINES
Gioia del Colle bianco (Puglia): dry white wine served at 50°F / 10°C
Colli Perugino bianco (Umbria): dry white wine served at 50°F / 10°C

1 Trim the prickly lettuce, removing the outer leaves and hard par
Wash it carefully and place in a salad bowl after lightly breaking th
leaves.

2 Clean the pepper, remove the stem and seeds and slice as thin
as possible. Cut the mozzarella into cubes.

3 Add the sliced pepper to the lettuce and add the choppe
mozzarella as well. Season everything with a bit of lemon juice,
small amount of olive oil and freshly ground pepper. Mix well an
serve.

PRACTICAL SUGGESTIONS
*Like all recipes that also rely on their aesthetic effect, you should be carefu
when selecting a serving dish for this salad. If you want a more unusua
flavor, you can use cubed tofu instead of the mozzarella; first scald it i
lightly salted boiling water acidulated with lemon juice.*

Bell Pepper Involtini

INGREDIENTS

serves 4

2 BELL PEPPERS (green, red, or gold)
1/2 oz. – 15 g RAISINS
1 clove GARLIC
1 sprig PARSLEY
2 ANCHOVIES IN SALT
1/2 oz. – 15 g CAPERS
STALE BREAD CRUMBS as necessary
1/2 oz. – 15 g PINE NUTS
SALT to taste
5 tablespoons EXTRA VIRGIN OLIVE OIL

EQUIPMENT

a bowl
a mixing bowl
a baking dish

Difficulty	**AVERAGE**
Preparation Time	**30 MIN.**
Cooking Time	**30 MIN.**
Method of cooking	**STOVETOP AND OVEN**
Microwave	**YES**
Freezing	**NO**
Keeping Time	**2 DAYS**

SPECIAL NOTE

The bark of the caper bush *(Capparis spinosa)* contains a bitter, irritating glycoside (capparirutin) that has diuretic, antiarthritic properties.

RECOMMENDED WINES
Martina Franca (Puglia): dry white wine served at 50°F / 10°C
Capri bianco (Campania): dry white wine served at 50°F / 10°C

1 Wash the bell peppers, dry well with a dishtowel and roast in a preheated 350°F oven for about 15 minutes, or until the skin begin to blacken.

2 In the meantime, prepare the other ingredients for the stuffing Place the raisins in a bowl of lukewarm water for 10 minutes, and peel the garlic. Wash and trim the parsley. Wash the anchovies eliminate the salt, and remove the backbone and head.

3 At this point, using a chopping knife, finely mince the parsley anchovies, garlic and capers together, and place in a mixing bow with the crumbled bread crumbs.

4 Finally, add the pine nuts, the well-squeezed raisins and a pinch of salt, and drizzle with 4 tablespoons oil, thoroughly mixing with wooden spoon to amalgamate the ingredients well.

5 When the green peppers are ready, skin them, remove the seeds and white part and cut them lengthwise. Place them in a baking dish greased with the remaining oil, stuff them with the prepared mixture and bake at 350°F for fifteen minutes, then serve.

PRACTICAL SUGGESTIONS

You can serve these bell peppers either hot or cold, as an appetizer or an accompaniment to a main course. They are also excellent baked the day before and stored in the refrigerator.

Savory Watercress Tart

INGREDIENTS

serves 4

1 lb. – 500 g WATERCRESS
1 SHALLOT
2 tablespoons SESAME OIL
SALT and PEPPER to taste
4 EGGS
2 oz. – 1 bunch PARSLEY

EQUIPMENT

a frying pan
a mixing bowl
a pie pan
a bowl
a serving dish

Difficulty	AVERAGE
Preparation Time	20 MIN.
Cooking Time	40 MIN.
Method of cooking	STOVETOP AND OVEN
Microwave	NO
Freezing	NO
Keeping Time	2 DAYS

SPECIAL NOTE

Since ancient times, watercress has been attributed with numerous therapeutic properties. It is rich in vitamins A, B and C and contains calcium, phosphorous and iron.

RECOMMENDED WINES
Grignolino d'Asti (Piedmont): light red wine served at 57°F / 14°C
Montepulciano d'Abruzzo Cerasuolo (Abruzzi): rosé served at 57 / 14°C°

1 Clean and thoroughly wash the watercress, then dry gently with a kitchen towel. Wilt the peeled, washed and minced shallot in a frying pan with the oil but do not allow it to brown. Add the watercress, stir with a wooden spoon and season with a pinch of salt and a dash of fresh pepper. Cover the frying pan and cook for about 10 minutes over moderate heat. Then remove the watercress from the frying pan, chop it coarsely, place it in a bowl and set aside.

2 Preheat the oven to 350°F. Using a fork, lightly beat the eggs in a bowl. Add the chopped watercress, the washed and minced parsley and a pinch of salt and freshly ground pepper. Mix the ingredients with a wooden spoon until perfectly blended.

3 Pour the mixture in a lightly oiled pie pan, place in the oven and bake about 25 minutes. Remove from the oven, turn out onto a serving dish and serve hot.

PRACTICAL SUGGESTIONS
In place of watercress, this delicious savory tart will be just as tasty if you use an equal amount of other wild or store-bought herbs.

Bell Pepper Involtini with Tuna

INGREDIENTS

serves 4

2 BELL PEPPERS
3 oz. – 70 g TUNA IN OLIVE OIL
half a LEMON
2 oz. – 1 bunch PARSLEY
2 oz. – 1 bunch TARRAGON
1 teaspoon CAPERS
2 PICKLES
2 EGG YOLKS
1 tablespoon EXTRA VIRGIN OLIVE OIL
SALT and WHITE PEPPER to taste
1 oz. – 20 g GRATED HORSERADISH ROOT

EQUIPMENT

a grill, a paper bag
a small bowl
a mixing bowl
a serving dish

Difficulty	AVERAGE
Preparation Time	40 MIN.
Cooking Time	10 MIN.
Method of cooking	GRILL
Microwave	NO
Freezing	NO
Keeping Time	2 DAYS

SPECIAL NOTE

Horseradish is known as *cren* in the Veneto, Friuli–Venezia Giulia and Alto Adige areas of Italy, where it can be bought in chunks that can be grated as necessary for use.

Recommended Wines
Colli Piacentini Ortrugo (Emilia Romagna):
dry white wine served at 50°F / 10°C
Colli Altotiberini bianco (Umbria): dry white wine served at 50°F / 10°C

1 Blacken the whole bell peppers over a grill, turning often. Place them in a paper bag and let them sit about 10 minutes. Remove the skin, seeds, and inner white portion and cut them into strips. Wash and dry with an extremely clean cloth.

2 Drain the tuna of its packing oil and mince it finely. Squeeze the lemon and place the juice in a small bowl. Wash the parsley and tarragon, dry with a clean cloth and finely mince with the capers and pickles, drained of their vinegar.

3 Place a pinch of salt and a few drops of lemon juice in a mixing bowl, add the egg yolks and mix. Drizzle in the oil drop by drop, stirring continuously in a clockwise direction. When the sauce begins to thicken, drizzle in the remaining oil, alternating with a few drops of lemon juice. When the oil is completely absorbed, season the sauce with a pinch of salt and freshly ground white pepper, then the remaining lemon juice.

4 Add the capers, pickles, tuna, parsley and tarragon, and blend the ingredients well. Spread a little of the mixture on each pepper slice and roll it up. Place the involtini on a serving dish and sprinkle with horseradish.

Practical Suggestions
If you want to make this dish even more appetizing, you can add 2 cleaned, boned and minced salted anchovies to the green pepper stuffing, or else a few minced olives.

Beef Carpaccio

INGREDIENTS
serves 4

3/4 lb. – 300 g BEEF TENDERLOIN
1 small BLACK TRUFFLE
1 stalk CELERY
3 tablespoons – 50 g PARMESAN CHEESE
6 oz. – 150 g MUSHROOMS
2 tablespoons LEMON JUICE
SALT and PEPPER to taste
4 tablespoons EXTRA VIRGIN OLIVE OIL
a few CORIANDER SEEDS

EQUIPMENT
a bowl
a serving dish

Difficulty	EASY
Preparation Time	25 MIN.
Cooking Time	NO
Method of cooking	NO
Microwave	NO
Freezing	NO
Keeping Time	1 DAY

SPECIAL NOTE
Carpaccio or carpacio, is a recently invented raw meat dish with a number of variations. It probably originated in the Veneto region, perhaps by Giuseppe Cipriani.

RECOMMENDED WINES
Salice Salentino rosato (Puglia): rosé served at 54°F / 12°C
Trentino Lagrein rosato (Trentino): rosé served at 54°F / 12°C

❖

1 Place the beef tenderloin in the freezer for under an hour until n◖ quite frozen. With a very sharp knife, slice the tenderloin against t◖ grain as paper-thin as possible.

2 Scrub the truffle, wash it quickly and slice thinly. Remove t◖ threads from the celery, wash it and chop. Slice the cheese. Remo◖ the hard, earthy portion of the mushrooms, wash them quick◖ under running water, drain, dry gently with a dishcloth and sli◖ thinly.

3 Place the lemon juice in a bowl with the salt and a pinch ◖ freshly ground pepper, and mix until the salt is completely dissolve◖ Add the oil and beat lightly with a fork until the sauce is we◖ emulsified.

4 Place the meat on a serving dish or individual plates. Place t◖ truffle, celery, cheese and mushrooms on it. Drizzle the carpacci◖ with the prepared sauce, sprinkle with coriander and serv◖ immediately.

PRACTICAL SUGGESTIONS
To conserve mushrooms, remember not to store them in a plastic bag; they last longer in a paper sack. To prevent them from discoloring after being slice◖ sprinkle them with a few drops of lemon juice.

Smoked Ham and Melon Drops

RECOMMENDED WINES

Oltrepò Pavese Moscato (Lombardy): aged red wine served at 46°F / 8°C
Aquileia del Friuli Chardonnay spumante (Friuli): liqueur-like wine or
sweet raisin wine served at 43°F / 6°C

Peel the cantaloupe, which should have been refrigerated, cut it half and remove the seeds and threads from the center. Using a melonballer or teaspoon, make as many small melon balls as you have slices of smoked ham.

On a flat surface, spread out the slices of ham and place a melon ball in the center of each one. Wrap the ham around it as if you were wrapping a candy. Place the "drops" on a serving dish and serve immediately before the ham grows soggy.

INGREDIENTS
serves 4

1 CANTALOUPE
4 oz. — 100 g SMOKED HAM
sliced very thinly

EQUIPMENT
a corer (melon ball cutter)
a serving dish

Difficulty	EASY
Preparation Time	20 MIN.
Cooking Time	NO
Method of cooking	NO
Microwave	NO
Freezing	NO
Keeping Time	1 DAY

SPECIAL NOTE
Smoked Tyrol ham, also known as *speck*, is produced in Alto Adige and Trentino, and is prepared using sides and haunches of pork that have been split, boned, salted, smoked and aged for 4—6 months.

PRACTICAL SUGGESTIONS
This enjoyable appetizer is especially suitable for a children's lunch, and is also good for using up any leftover melon. If you like, you can season the cantaloupe with a pinch of salt and freshly ground white pepper.

rostini Valle d'Aosta-Style   p72

Spinach Tarlets   p73

armesan Croquettes   p74

Cheese in Pastry   p76

tuffed Polenta Rounds   p78

Drunken Squash   p80

Cheese Torte   p82

heese and Ham Paté   p84

Eggs with Mushroom Sauce   p85

Fall and Winter Antipasti

Eggs with Caviar

INGREDIENTS

serves 4

4 EGGS
2 BLOOD ORANGES
SALT to taste
4 tablespoons PLAIN YOGURT
1 jar CAVIAR

EQUIPMENT

a skillet
a serving dish

Difficulty	EASY
Preparation Time	15 MIN.
Cooking Time	10 MIN.
Method of cooking	STOVETOP
Microwave	NO
Freezing	NO
Keeping Time	1 DAY

SPECIAL NOTE

According to legend, yogurt, which was known to Asiatic nomadic shepherds in ancient times, reached Europe in 1542 through the French ambassador in Constantinople.

RECOMMENDED WINES

Franciacorta Spumante (Lombardy): liqueur–like wine or sweet raisin wine served at 43°F / 6°C
Prosecco di Valdobbiadene Superiore di Cartizze (Veneto): liqueur–like wine or sweet raisin wine served at 43°F / 6°C

1 Immerse the eggs (which should be at room temperature to prevent them from breaking during cooking) in a skillet with generous amount of water and bring to a boil over moderate heat. After 5 minutes, drain them, run under cold water and peel.

2 Slice off enough of the bottom of the eggs to allow them to stand upright, then arrange on a serving dish and cut them vertically to halfway down, so they will open without separating completely.

3 Cut the oranges into slices and place a slice under each egg. Salt the inside of the egg, place a tablespoon of yogurt in each one and then a teaspoon of caviar, forming a strip, and serve.

PRACTICAL SUGGESTIONS

Before adding the yogurt to the eggs, you can add a tablespoon of vodka to it, mix well, and proceed as indicated in the recipe. Like all dishes where oranges are served with the peel, use untreated fruit if you can.

Little Cheese Pears

RECOMMENDED WINES

Valle Isarco Traminer aromatico (Trentino–Alto Adige): mellow, aromatic white wine served at 50°F / 10°C
Roero (Piedmont): light red wine served at 57°F / 16°C

Bring the milk to a boil in a small saucepan. In a skillet, mix the flour (setting aside one tablespoon) with the parmesan and gruyère, seasoned with salt and pepper, add the two eggs, and then the egg yolks, one at a time. Add the boiling milk, drizzling it in. Place over moderate heat and gently bring to a boil, stirring constantly. Boil for a minute, remove from the heat, add 1 oz. – 20 grams butter and blend well.

Butter a flat surface, pour the mixture on it, and spread with a spatula into a layer almost 1 inch – 2 centimeters thick, and allow to cool. When it has completely cooled, form it into little pear shapes with lightly floured hands (using the flour you set aside). Before sure to flatten the base so they will stand upright.

Trim the carrot, peel, cut into little matchstick–sized strips and place in the center of the pear to form the stem. When time to serve, beat the remaining egg, dip the pears in it a few at a time, roll them in bread crumbs and fry in a frying pan in a generous amount of hot but not boiling peanut oil. Drain on a paper towel, place on a serving dish and serve hot.

PRACTICAL SUGGESTIONS

This original recipe (adapted from a children's snack) can be varied as you like. For example, you can add 3 oz – 100 grams finely minced ham to the dough, or else leftover minced roast or braised meat.

INGREDIENTS
serves 6

2 cups – 1/2 liter MILK
1 1/4 cups – 160 g WHITE FLOUR
3 tablespoons – 60 g GRATED PARMESAN CHEESE
3 tablespoons – 60 g GRATED GRUYÈRE
SALT and PEPPER to taste
3 EGGS
5 EGG YOLKS
1/4 cup – 40 g BUTTER
1 CARROT
2 tablespoons BREAD CRUMBS
PEANUT OIL for frying

EQUIPMENT
a small saucepan, a skillet
a frying pan, a serving dish
absorbent paper towels

Difficulty	AVERAGE
Preparation Time	30 MIN.
Cooking Time	25 MIN.
Method of cooking	STOVETOP
Microwave	NO
Freezing	YES
Keeping Time	2 DAYS

SPECIAL NOTE
Peanut oil contains polyunsaturated fatty acids, and is thus indicated for the prevention and treatment of illnesses related to arteriosclerosis (heart attacks, arterial diseases, etc.).

Chard Pockets

INGREDIENTS

serves 4

half a LEMON
2.2 lb. – I kg SWISS CHARD
I tablespoon WHITE FLOUR
SALT to taste
6 oz. – 150 g FONTINA CHEESE
2 EGGS
2 tablespoons BREAD CRUMBS
PEANUT OIL for frying

EQUIPMENT

2 bowls
a skillet
a frying pan
absorbent paper towels
a serving dish

Difficulty	AVERAGE
Preparation Time	15 MIN.
Cooking Time	30 MIN.
Method of cooking	STOVETOP
Microwave	NO
Freezing	YES
Keeping Time	3 DAYS

SPECIAL NOTE

Italian law requires that the name "fontina" can be used only for cheese produced in Valle d'Aosta. Similar cheeses produced in other regions are referred to as "fontal."

Recommended Wines
Valle d'Aosta rosato (Valle d'Aosta): rosé served at 54°F / 12°C
Candia dei Colli Apuani (Tuscany): dry white wine served at 50°F / 10°C

I Squeeze the lemon, collect the juice in a bowl and set it aside Separate the chard stalks from the green leaves (which you can use for other dishes), remove the threads and cut into pieces about : inches – 8 centimeters long, wash thoroughly and drain.

2 In a skillet, dissolve the flour in a little cold water, add the lemon juice, a generous amount of water and a pinch of salt, and add the pieces of chard. Slowly bring to a boil and cook about 7–8 minutes Drain onto a dishcloth and dry.

3 Remove the rind from the cheese and cut it into slices the same size as the chard. Lightly beat the eggs in a bowl with a pinch of salt Place the chard on a flat surface, and place the cheese slices on half of them. Cover with the remaining chard to form sandwiches. Dip into the beaten eggs and the roll in bread crumbs.

4 Fry the pockets in a frying pan with a generous amount of hot bu not boiling oil, until they are browned. Drain onto a paper towel transfer to a serving dish and serve hot.

Practical Suggestions
You can prepare little dumplings with the Swiss chard leaves you did no use. Boil them, then blend them with 3/4 lb. – 300 g ricotta, 2 eggs and 5 tablespoons grated parmesan, dip in flour and fry in hot oil.

Savory Polenta Rounds

INGREDIENTS

serves 4

1 PACKAGE QUICK–COOKING POLENTA (or grits)
10 SLICES PROCESSED CHEESE
4 tablespoons EXTRA VIRGIN OLIVE OIL
1 lb. – 400 g TOMATO PURÉE
1 clove GARLIC
2 oz. – 1 bunch BASIL or PARSLEY
SALT to taste

EQUIPMENT

a pot
a saucepan
a baking dish

Difficulty	AVERAGE
Preparation Time	15 MIN.
Cooking Time	40 MIN.
Method of cooking	STOVETOP AND OVEN
Microwave	YES
Freezing	NO
Keeping Time	2 DAYS

SPECIAL NOTE

As early as 1578, corn (maize) was mentioned in the writings of the Chinese Li-ti-Chin, while in ancient Central Asia and Turkey, it was considered a blessing from heaven.

RECOMMENDED WINES
Bardolino Novello (Veneto): rosé served at 54°F / 12°C
Bolgheri rosato (Tuscany): rosé served at 54°F / 12°C

❖

1 Prepare the polenta according to the instructions on the package. After about 10 minutes, turn it out onto a slightly damp flat surface and push it out to a thickness of a little under 1/2 inch – centimeter, then let it cool. Preheat the oven to 400°F.

2 Cut the cheese slices into little pieces and prepare the sauce. Place the olive oil, the tomato purée and a clove of peeled, washed garlic into a saucepan, and cook at high heat for about 15 minutes. Remove the garlic, add the washed and dried basil and salt, and remove from the heat.

3 Using a glass with a dampened edge, cut out rounds from the polenta. Place them in a baking dish, slightly overlapping, with a bit of oil. Place the cheese and prepared sauce on them. Bake about ten minutes and serve immediately.

PRACTICAL SUGGESTIONS
This hearty winter appetizer works especially well for leftover polenta. Canned tomato purée will work very well here.

52

Cheese Puffs

INGREDIENTS

serves 4

1 oz. – 20 g BUTTER
1 tablespoon – 20 g WHITE FLOUR
1 cup – 1/4 liter MILK
3 tablespoons – 1 dl CREAM
SALT and WHITE PEPPER to taste
6 oz. – 70 g EMMENTAL CHEESE
2 oz. – 50 g MILD GORGONZOLA
2 EGG YOLKS
18 PUFF PASTRIES

EQUIPMENT

a pastry bag
a saucepan

Difficulty	**AVERAGE**
Preparation Time	**15 MIN.**
Cooking Time	**20 MIN.**
Method of cooking	**STOVETOP AND OVEN**
Microwave	**YES**
Freezing	**NO**
Keeping Time	**2 DAYS**

SPECIAL NOTE

Gorgonzola is characterized by marbling, the bluish veins induced by *Penicillium weidmannii* mold, which is artificially injected into the forms.

RECOMMENDED WINES
Freisa d'Asti (Piedmont): light red wine served at 57°F / 14°C
Orvieto classico (Umbria): mellow, aromatic white wine served at 50°F / 10°C

1 Melt the butter in a saucepan, add the sifted flour, and sauté for a few minutes, stirring constantly. Add the milk and cream and mix with a wooden spoon to blend well. Bring to a boil and season with a pinch of salt and freshly ground white pepper.

2 Continue cooking for 7–8 minutes, then add the cheeses chopped into small pieces, and mix until they are completely melted. Add the egg yolks one by one, blending them perfectly with the mixture.

3 Pour the cheese cream into a pastry bag and fill the pastries. Before eating them, place them in a preheated 320°F oven, and serve hot or tepid.

PRACTICAL SUGGESTIONS
This dish also gives excellent results if you use other kinds of sharp or mild cheese, depending on whether you prefer a delicate or more pungent flavor. Of course, you can also use leftover cheese.

Mushroom Strudel

INGREDIENTS

serves 4

1 LB. – 500 G FRESH MUSHROOMS, preferably porcini

2 oz. – 1 bunch TARRAGON or PARSLEY

2 1/2 cups – 300 g WHITE FLOUR

1.5 OZ. – 30 G BREAD CRUMBS

1/2 OZ. – 15 G SUGAR

1 EGG

1 LEEK

1/2 cup – 110 g BUTTER

SALT to taste

EQUIPMENT

a skillet

a baking sheet

a serving dish

Difficulty	AVERAGE
Preparation Time	40 MIN.
Cooking Time	50 MIN.
Method of cooking	STOVETOP AND OVEN
Microwave	YES
Freezing	YES
Keeping Time	2 DAYS

SPECIAL NOTE

Ibnal Baithar, a 13th century Arabic botanist, claimed that tarragon freshened the breath, and that it would make medicine more palatable when chewed first.

1 Trim the mushrooms, clean them with a damp towel and slice. Trim the leek and tarragon, then slice the former and mince the latter. Place the mushrooms in a skillet with 1 oz. butter and the leek and cook for 20 minutes.

2 Mound 2 1/3 cups – 280 grams flour on a cutting board and break the egg in the center. Add 1/3 cup butter – 80 grams flaked butter, the sugar and salt, and blend and work the ingredients, adding a bit of lukewarm water, until you have a firm dough. Roll it out to a thin layer and cut out rounds about 4 inches – 10 centimeters in diameter.

3 Finish cooking the mushrooms, add the tarragon, sprinkle in the remaining flour, and add a pinch of salt. Mix well with a wooden spoon, and as soon as everything is well–blended, remove the pan from the heat. Sprinkle the rounds with bread crumbs and spread the mushrooms on them, leaving the edges free.

4 Form little caps from the rounds by lifting the edges at various points and pinching shut. Place them on a buttered baking sheet. Bake the strudel at 350°F for about a half an hour, then remove, transfer to a serving dish and serve either tepid or cold.

PRACTICAL SUGGESTIONS

To speed up preparation time for these exquisite strudels, you can buy prepared phyllo dough. If you want to make the mushroom mixture more delicate, add a small cup of béchamel sauce.

Fried Cauliflower with Sauce

INGREDIENTS

serves 4

1 CAULIFLOWER (about 2 lb. — 800 g)
3 EGGS
2 cups — 250 g WHITE FLOUR
SALT and PEPPER to taste
2 SALTED ANCHOVIES
SESAME or OLIVE OIL for frying
6 tablespoons — 2 dl TOMATO SAUCE

EQUIPMENT

a pot
a mixing bowl
a frying pan
absorbent paper towels
a serving dish

Difficulty	AVERAGE
Preparation Time	15 MIN.
Cooking Time	20 MIN.
Method of cooking	STOVETOP
Microwave	NO
Freezing	NO
Keeping Time	2 DAYS

SPECIAL NOTE

In international cuisine, cauliflower dishes are referred to as "alla Dubarry," from the name of Louis XV's favorite, who is said to have been particularly fond of cauliflower.

Recommended Wines
Grignolino d'Asti (Piedmont): light red wine served at 57°F / 14°C
Verdicchio (Marche): dry white wine served at 50°F / 10°C

1 Break the cauliflower into medium–sized florets and cook in a pan of salted water. Drain, cool and set aside. Break the eggs into mixing bowl, beat them lightly and add the flour a little at a time mixing to prevent it from clumping, and add a little water if necessary.

2 Add a pinch of salt and freshly ground pepper to the batter. Wash the anchovies very well, remove the head and backbone, cut into little pieces and add to the batter. Heat a generous amount of oil in a frying pan and add the cauliflower flowerets.

3 Immerse the florets into the hot oil, browning them uniformly. Drain and place on paper towels to absorb any excess oil. Serve hot on a serving dish, accompanied by the tomato sauce.

Practical Suggestions
You can cook the cauliflower florets in water acidulated with vinegar including apple cider vinegar. You will not only obtain a more pronounced flavor, but you will also greatly reduce the bad odor cauliflower emits when cooking. Something else you can do to eliminate this is to add a piece of dry bread or biscuit to the cooking water, or cover the pot cover with a cloth soaked in vinegar, which will "filter" the steam.

Onion and Vodka Crostini

INGREDIENTS

serves 4

2 lb. – 800 g ONIONS
3 tablespoons EXTRA VIRGIN OLIVE OIL
2 cups VEGETABLE BROTH
1 cup VODKA
8 SLICES HOMEMADE BREAD
4–5 tablespoons PEANUT OIL

EQUIPMENT

a skillet
a frying pan
a slotted spatula
absorbent paper towels
a serving dish

Difficulty	**AVERAGE**
Preparation Time	**15 MIN.**
Cooking Time	**40 MIN.**
Method of cooking	**STOVETOP**
Microwave	**YES**
Freezing	**NO**
Keeping Time	**1 DAY**

SPECIAL NOTE

By soaking an equal amount of fresh onion pulp in alcohol at 194°F for 10 days, you will obtain a tincture that can be used as a diuretic, to lower blood sugar, and as an antiseptic.

Recommended Wines
Lambrusco Reggiano rosato (Emilia–Romagna): rosé served at 54°F / 12°
Castel del Monte rosato (Puglia): rosé served at 54°F / 12°

1 Clean, wash and slice the onions, the cook over low heat in skillet of olive oil and about a half a cup of vegetable broth.

2 When they are tender (about 30 minutes), drizzle with vodk increase the heat to evaporate the alcohol, and as soon as they hav absorbed the cooking liquid, remove from the heat.

3 Lightly moisten the slices of homemade bread with the brotl then fry them in a frying pan with peanut oil. Remove with a slotte spatula and place on a paper towel to absorb any excess oil. Place spoonful of onions on each slice, transfer the croutons to a servin dish and serve hot.

Practical Suggestions
This appetizer makes an especially good beginning for a rustic lunch or meal in the country. Of course, if you don't have vodka, you can als obtain excellent results with dry white wine.

Egg and Mushroom Crostini

RECOMMENDED WINES
Aglianico del Taburno rosato (Campania): rosé served at 54°F / 12°C
Bolgheri rosato (Tuscany): rosé served at 54°F / 12°C

Cut the rolls in half horizontally, place them on a lightly oiled ⸺king sheet and place a spoonful of tomato sauce on each one.

Remove the earthy, hard portion from the mushrooms, wash ⸺em quickly, dry and slice. Place them in a saucepan with the oil ⸺d the clove of garlic and cook 15–20 minutes. When cooked, salt ⸺d pepper them, add the remaining tomato sauce, remove the garlic ⸺d mix to completely blend the ingredients.

In a saucepan, boil the water with the vinegar and a pinch of salt. ⸺eak the eggs into a bowl, and drop them one by one into the ⸺oiling water. Cook about 3 minutes, or until the white has covered ⸺e yolk. Remove with a slotted spoon and place on a dry dishcloth.

Cut the mozzarella into four thin slices. Place an egg on each half ⸺ll, cover with the mushroom sauce, place a slice of mozzarella on ⸺p, and bake in a 340°F oven for 15 minutes. Serve hot.

PRACTICAL SUGGESTIONS
⸺hese big croutons will be even more tasty if you use an equal amount of ⸺rcini mushrooms instead of the champignon mushrooms. You can also ⸺ake them elegant by using rectangular slices of bread cut into special ⸺apes, instead of the rolls.

INGREDIENTS
serves 4

2 ROUND ROLLS
8 tablespoons TOMATO SAUCE
1/2 lb. – 200 g CHAMPIGNON MUSHROOMS
2 tablespoons EXTRA VIRGIN OLIVE OIL
1 clove GARLIC
1 tablespoon VINEGAR
SALT and PEPPER to taste
4 EGGS
6 oz. – 80 g FRESH MOZZARELLA

EQUIPMENT
a saucepan
a small saucepan
a baking sheet

Difficulty	AVERAGE
Preparation Time	10 MIN.
Cooking Time	50 MIN.
Method of cooking	STOVETOP AND OVEN
Microwave	YES
Freezing	NO
Keeping Time	1 DAY

SPECIAL NOTE
Champignon is a French word that means "mushroom," and is internationally used to indicate the most common type of cultivated mushroom, in its white and "blond" varieties, i.e. the button mushroom.

Harlequin Antipasti

INGREDIENTS

serves 4

2 GRANNY SMITH APPLES
2 ORANGES
8 oz. – 200 g CANNED TUNA
10 QUAIL EGGS
3 tablespoons EXTRA VIRGIN OLIVE OIL
SALT to taste
4 STALKS CELERY
juice of HALF A LEMON
1 oz. – 20 g PINE NUTS

EQUIPMENT

a mixing bowl
a small bowl
a skillet
4 small glass serving cups

Difficulty	**EASY**
Preparation Time	**15 MIN.**
Cooking Time	**4–5 MIN.**
Method of cooking	**STOVETOP**
Microwave	**NO**
Freezing	**NO**
Keeping Time	**1 DAY**

SPECIAL NOTE

The female quail lays from 7 to 12 eggs, which she broods in a grass-lined hollow in the ground. She may lay two clutches of eggs in one summer.

RECOMMENDED WINES
Colli Orientali del Friuli Sauvignon (Friuli): mellow, aromatic white win
served at 50°F / 10°C
Oltrepò Pavese Riesling Renano (Lombardy): dry white wine
served at 50°F / 10°C

1 Peel the apples and oranges, slice them thinly and place in mixing bowl. Using a fork, crumble the tuna. Trim the celery, wash and cut into rounds. Add the tuna and celery to the sliced fruit.

2 Fill a skillet with water, bring to a boil and hardboil the quail egg for a few minutes, then peel, cut in half and place in the bowl wit the other ingredients.

3 Beat the oil in a small bowl with a pinch of salt and the lemo juice. Blend well, and use this dressing to season the salad. Mix we and place in individual serving cups, decorating with a teaspoon o pine nuts

PRACTICAL SUGGESTIONS

You can use chicken eggs instead of quail eggs. If you do, use only instead of 10. Remember that quail eggs hardboil in just a few minutes.

Rice Tart with Fontina Cheese

INGREDIENTS

serves 4

For the crust

1 1/4 cup — 150 g WHITE FLOUR

1/3 cup — 75 g BUTTER

1 EGG YOLK

SALT to taste

For the filling

2 LEEKS

1/8 cup — 30 g BUTTER

1/4 lb. — 100 g RICE

1/2 cup DRY WHITE WINE

VEGETABLE BROTH as necessary

1/2 lb. — 200 g FONTINA CHEESE

SALT and PEPPER to taste

EQUIPMENT

a skillet

a 9.5 inch — 24 cm pie pan

Difficulty	**AVERAGE**
Preparation Time	**20 MIN. + 1 HOUR**
Cooking Time	**50 MIN.**
Method of cooking	**STOVETOP AND OVEN**
Microwave	**YES**
Freezing	**NO**
Keeping Time	**2 DAYS**

SPECIAL NOTE

Rice has a protein content similar to bread, but rice protein is more similar to animal protein and is thus more nutritious and easier for our tissues to assimilate.

RECOMMENDED WINES

Barbera d'Alba (Piedmont): light red wine served at 61°F / 16°C

Cellatica (Lombardy): light red wine served at 61°F / 16°C

1 Prepare the crust: sift the flour and salt onto a cutting board. In the center, place the chopped butter, the egg yolk and 2 tablespoon water. Using your fingertips, quickly work the mixture, then form ball, wrap in a cloth and chill for an hour.

2 Trim the roots from the leeks and remove the hard outer leave then slice into thin rounds, wash and dry. Place in a skillet with the butter and sauté at moderate heat, then add the rice, and stirring toast for 2 minutes. Add the wine and let it evaporate, then add the hot broth a little at a time and continue cooking for 15 minute stirring from time to time.

3 In the meantime, preheat the oven to 350°F. When the rice ready and rather dry, remove from the heat, let it grow lukewarm and then, continuing to mix, add the eggs, the cubed fontina, fresh ground pepper, and salt if necessary.

4 Roll the dough out thinly and place in the buttered pie pan. Pric the dough with a fork and then add the prepared mixture, spread evenly and bake for 30 minutes. Serve hot or lukewarm.

PRACTICAL SUGGESTIONS

This rich appetizer (which could also be a first course) is particularly goo for using up leftover rice. If you don't have fontina cheese, you ca substitute any other cheese you like.

Fra' Guglielmo Salad

INGREDIENTS

serves 4

2 lb. – 800 g FENNEL
1/4 lb. – 100 g SHARP GORGONZOLA
2 tablespoons EXTRA VIRGIN OLIVE OIL
1 espresso cup CREAM
SALT and PEPPER to taste
1 sprig PARSLEY

EQUIPMENT

a bowl
a serving dish

Difficulty	EASY
Preparation Time	20 MIN.
Cooking Time	NO
Method of cooking	NO
Microwave	NO
Freezing	NO
Keeping Time	1 DAY

SPECIAL NOTE

Herbalists use fennel roots, which have diuretic properties, and the fruit, which is commonly and improperly referred to as seeds.

Recommended Wines
Taburno rosato (Campania): rosé served at 54°F / 12°C
Dolcetto d'Asti (Piedmont): light red wine served at 57°F / 14°C

1 Carefully trim the fennel, wash them well under running water and cut them in half and then in quarters. Place them on a fl. working surface and slice them very thinly horizontally. Arrang these slices on the bottom of a serving dish, then go on to prepar the sauce.

2 Crumble the gorgonzola with a fork and place in a bowl. Slowl moisten it with olive oil, and then add the cream. Mix it well with wooden spoon until it becomes creamy (if the mixture is too dry, ad more cream and oil). Finally, salt moderately and season with a pinch o freshly ground pepper. Spread the mixture on the fennel.

3 Trim, wash and dry the parsley, then, using a chopping knife mince it very finely, sprinkle it on and serve.

Practical Suggestions
If you want a more delicate flavor, use mild rather than sharp gorgonzol In this case, you should reduce the amount of cream.

66

Pecorino Bundles

INGREDIENTS

serves 4

1 lb. – 400 g PLUM TOMATOES
3/4 lb. – 300 BREAD DOUGH, already risen
3/4 lb. – 350 g FRESH PECORINO CHEESE
OLIVE OIL as necessary
SALT and PEPPER to taste

EQUIPMENT

a rolling pin
a frying pan
absorbent paper towels
a serving dish

Difficulty	AVERAGE
Preparation Time	20 MIN.
Cooking Time	20 MIN.
Method of cooking	STOVETOP
Microwave	NO
Freezing	YES
Keeping Time	2 DAYS

SPECIAL NOTE

Pecorino (sheep cheese) has 36% fat and is aged for at least eight months in natural temperature storehouses known in Italian as *caciare*. The cheese is produced in the fall and winter.

RECOMMENDED WINES
Biferno rosato (Molise): rosé served at 54°F / 12°C
Castel del Monte rosato (Puglia): rosé served at 54°F / 12°C

❖

1 Scald the tomatoes for 2 minutes in boiling water, drain an remove the skin, seeds and vegetable water, then chop coarsely an set aside.

2 Roll out the dough on a lightly floured surface to a thickness c about 3/16 inch – 4–5 millimeters. Using a wide cup, cut ou numerous rounds about 4 inches – 10 centimeters in diameter.

3 Place the tomato, cubed pecorino, a bit of oil and a pinch of sa and freshly ground pepper on each round. Close the rounds b forming half moons and pressing firmly to seal the edges.

4 Fry the bundles in a frying pan with a generous amount of hot oi a few at a time, until they are puffy and golden brown. Drain on paper towel, transfer to a serving dish and serve hot.

PRACTICAL SUGGESTIONS
These tasty bundles make an excellent first course for a winter lunch, but ar equally good as an accompaniment to aperitifs.

Crostini with Apple and Horseradish Cream

INGREDIENTS

serves 4

1 APPLE, 1 small piece HORSERADISH,
3 tablespoons CREAM OR
LOW-FAT YOGURT
2 tablespoons RAW CANE SUGAR
YOGURT, 2 tablespoons BREAD CRUMBS
3 tablespoons APPLE CIDER VINEGAR
8 slices RYE BREAD

EQUIPMENT

a mixing bowl
a small bowl
a small saucepan
a serving dish

Difficulty	EASY
Preparation Time	15 MIN.
Cooking Time	NO
Method of cooking	NO
Microwave	NO
Freezing	NO
Keeping Time	1 DAY

SPECIAL NOTE

Horseradish, a native of southeast Europe, reach medieval monasteries around the year 1000 and immediately gained popularity. At the time, it was prescribed for kidney stones.

RECOMMENDED WINES

Capriano del Colle Trebbiano (Lombardy): dry white wine served at 50°F / 10°
Alto Adige Pinot grigio (Alto Adige): dry white wine served at 50°F / 10°

❖

1 Peel the apple, remove the core and cut in half. Grate the first h. and place into a small bowl. Cook the other half in a small saucep of water, then sieve.

2 Scrub the horseradish well and then grate it finely. Place in mixing bowl and add the cream or nonfat yogurt, the prepared appl the sugar, the bread crumbs and the vinegar. Mix everything very w with a wooden spoon until it becomes soft and creamy.

3 Toast the slices of rye bread in the oven, then spread with t prepared mixture. Place the crostini on a serving dish and serve.

PRACTICAL SUGGESTIONS

If you don't like the distinctive taste of horseradish, you can use a small pie of ginger root instead, which has an equally pungent but less spicy flavor.

70

Valle d'Aosta–Style Crostini

INGREDIENTS

serves 4

I loaf stale WHOLE WHEAT BREAD
several teaspoons ACACIA HONEY
8 slices LARD (genuine, veined with red)
BLACK PEPPER to taste

EQUIPMENT

a serving dish

RECOMMENDED WINES

Valle d'Aosta rosso (Valle d'Aosta): light red wine served at 57°F / 14°C
Oltrepò Pavese Barbera (Lombardy): light red wine served at 61°F / 16°C

I Preheat the oven to 300°F. Cut the loaf of bread (be sure it's stale but not hard) into eight thin slices. Place them on the oven broiler and toast them lightly, then remove from the oven and place on a rather large serving dish.

2 Spread a thin layer of acacia honey on the slices of bread, then place a slice of lard on each one (the lard should be cut as thinly as possible). Finally, sprinkle with a pinch of freshly ground black pepper and serve.

Difficulty	EASY
Preparation Time	I0 MIN.
Cooking Time	NO
Method of cooking	NO
Microwave	NO
Freezing	NO
Keeping Time	2 DAYS

SPECIAL NOTE

Honey is extremely high in calories, as it contains two sugars, glucose and fructose, which the body can directly absorb.

PRACTICAL SUGGESTIONS

Red–veined lard, a specialty of several areas in Valle d'Aosta, which produces excellent lard, is particularly suitable for these simple, savory crostini. However, bacon may also be used. They can be used as an appetizer or, in larger quantities, as an unusual second course.

Spinach Tartlets

RECOMMENDED WINES
Riviera Ligure di Ponente Pigato (Liguria):
dry white wine served at 50°F / 10°C
Soave (Veneto): dry white wine served at 50°F / 10°Co °C

In a pot with a very small amount of lightly salted water, boil the trimmed, washed and drained spinach, then squeeze well and mince finely. Wash the anchovies well, remove the head and backbone, then break into pieces. Preheat the oven to 300°F.

Melt the butter in a frying pan, add the spinach and anchovies and cook for a few minutes, then add the cream and grated parmesan and continue cooking for a few minutes, stirring constantly with a wooden spoon to thoroughly blend the ingredients.

In the meantime, toast the bread in a hot oven, either leaving the square slices as they are, or cutting them in the form you prefer (if you can cut them into rounds, they will be very effective).

As soon as the slices are ready, butter them, spread with the spinach mixture and serve hot on a serving dish.

INGREDIENTS
serves 4

SALT to taste
1 lb. – 400 g SPINACH
1/8 cup – 30 g BUTTER
3 SALTED ANCHOVIES
5 tablespoons – 50 g CREAM
3 tablespoons – 60 g GRATED PARMESAN
8 square SLICES BREAD

EQUIPMENT
a pot
a frying pan
a serving dish

Difficulty	AVERAGE
Preparation Time	20 MIN.
Cooking Time	15 MIN.
Method of cooking	STOVETOP
Microwave	NO
Freezing	NO
Keeping Time	1 DAY

PRACTICAL SUGGESTIONS
If you want to give this preparation a more pronounced, original flavor, you can use 2 oz. – 50 grams plain low-fat yogurt instead of the cream. These excellent tarts will also work very well as a children's snack.

SPECIAL NOTE
Cream is the fatty part of milk, and is now obtained industrially using centrifugal cream separators. Commercial cream is obtained from cow's milk.

Parmesan Croquettes

INGREDIENTS

serves 4

1 2/3 cups — 200 g WHITE FLOUR
10 tablespoons — 200 g GRATED PARMESAN
SALT and PEPPER to taste
8 EGGS
2 cups — 1/2 liter MILK
1/8 cup — 30 g BUTTER
BREAD CRUMBS as necessary
SUNFLOWER SEED OIL for frying
or else peanut or sesame oil

EQUIPMENT

a skillet
a mixing bowl
a frying pan
absorbent paper towels

Difficulty	AVERAGE
Preparation Time	15 MIN.
Cooking Time	30 MIN.
Method of cooking	STOVETOP
Microwave	NO
Freezing	YES
Keeping Time	2 DAYS

SPECIAL NOTE

After parmesan has been aged, the forms are
struck with a special hammer that uses resonance
to indicate compactness and quality.

1 Place the flour in a skillet, add the grated parmesan, a pinch of
salt and freshly ground pepper, 6 egg yolks (setting the whites aside)
and 2 whole eggs. Mix everything well with a wooden spoon and
dilute with milk. Cover over moderate heat until the mixture
becomes quite thick.

2 Remove the skillet from the heat, add 1/8 cup — 30 grams butter,
mix again to blend the other ingredients, pour into a mixing bowl and
cool.

3 In the meantime, beat the egg whites in a dish. When the cheese
cream is cool, remove a spoonful at a time and form croquettes. Flour
them and dip into the beaten egg whites and then the bread crumbs.

4 Fry the croquettes in a frying pan with a generous amount of oil
and then place them on absorbent paper towels to eliminate any
excess oil. Serve hot or cold.

PRACTICAL SUGGESTIONS

*For these croquettes to be successful, you should fry them in abundant hot
oil (at least 2 cups — 0.5 liter), or else they will not be well-browned and
crispy. Accompanied by a fresh mixed vegetable salad or seasonal
vegetables sautéed in a frying pan with a bit of oil, they make an excellent
single-dish meal.*

Cheese in Pastry

INGREDIENTS

serves 4–6

1 3/4 cups – 200 g WHITE FLOUR
SALT and PEPPER to taste
plus 2 tablespoons
1/4 cup – 40 g BUTTER
1/2 lb. – 250 g MIXED CHEESES
2 cups MILK
1/2 OZ. – 15 G BAKER'S YEAST
3 EGGS

EQUIPMENT

a mixing bowl
a saucepan
a bowl
a baking dish

Difficulty	AVERAGE
Preparation Time	30 MIN. + 1 HOUR
Cooking Time	30 MIN.
Method of cooking	STOVETOP AND OVEN
Microwave	YES
Freezing	NO
Keeping Time	1 DAY

SPECIAL NOTE

Baker's yeast is used to make bread, and is most active between 50°F and 68°F. When fresh, it is light yellow and has a doughy consistency, and will keep for only a short time.

RECOMMENDED WINES
Piave Verduzzo (Veneto): dry white wine served at 50°F / 10°C
Alcamo (Sicily): dry white wine served at 50°F / 10°C

1 Mound 1 3/4 cups – 200 grams flour on a cutting board, add the crumbled yeast and a cup of lukewarm water. Add a pinch of salt and knead well until you have a smooth, firm dough. Cover it with damp cloth and let it rise for about an hour. Then place the dough in a mixing bowl, blend in all but a walnut-sized chunk of the butter then place it in a buttered baking dish, spreading it out to completely cover the bottom and sides.

2 Cut the cheeses into pieces, place them in a saucepan and, while cold, add 2 tablespoons flour and a cup of milk. Mix, add a pinch of pepper and cook over low heat, continuing to stir with a wooden spoon until the sauce has thickened.

3 At this point, add the 3 egg yolks one by one, blend them well and remove the saucepan from the heat. Whip the 3 egg whites to peaks in a bowl and gently fold them into the mixture.

4 Spread the cheese sauce on the dough and place the baking dish in the oven at moderate heat. When the surface is quite puffy remove from the oven and serve immediately.

PRACTICAL SUGGESTIONS
You can use any cheese you like for this recipe, provided it melts well. Some examples are mozzarella, ricotta, and grated parmesan. You can also add oz. – 100 g cubed ham.

Stuffed Polenta Rounds

INGREDIENTS

serves 4

3 oz. – 80 g ANCHOVIES IN OIL
1/8 cup – 30 g BUTTER
3/4 lb. – 300 g POLENTA
already prepared
I EGG
WHITE FLOUR as necessary
PEANUT OIL for frying

EQUIPMENT

a bowl
a round pasta cutter I I/4 inch – 3 cm in
diameter
a frying pan
absorbent paper towels

Difficulty	AVERAGE
Preparation Time	15 MIN.
Cooking Time	20 MIN.
Method of cooking	STOVETOP
Microwave	NO
Freezing	NO
Keeping Time	2 DAYS

SPECIAL NOTE

In 1556, Giovanni Lauro, a Cremona noble, gave
the Duke of Florence a certain quantity of corn,
assuring him that "it makes excellent polenta": so
good that it became the polenta par excellence.

RECOMMENDED WINES
Trebbiano di Romagna (Emilia Romagna):
dry white wine served at 50°F / 10°C
Parrina rosato (Tuscany): rosé served at 54°F / 12°C

1 Finely mince the anchovies, place in a bowl with the butt
softened to room temperature, and blend everything with
wooden spoon.

2 Cut the polenta into slices a little less than 1/4 inch – 5
millimeters thick. Using a round pasta cutter or a glass, for
numerous rounds 1 1/4 –1 1/2 inches – 3–4 centimeters in diamet

3 Spread the inner part of each round with a bit of the anchovy a
butter mixture, then make sandwiches with each one. Continue ur
you have finished the polenta.

4 Dip the sandwiches into the beaten egg and then the flour, then
them a few at a time in a frying pan with a generous amount of hot c
for 2–3 minutes, until they are lightly browned. Transfer to absorbe
paper towels to eliminate any extra oil.

PRACTICAL SUGGESTIONS
*These savory polenta sandwiches, which will be a great success wi
children, are an ideal way to reuse leftover polenta. If you want them to
lighter, you can brown them in a hot oven rather than breading and fryi
them.*

Drunken Squash

INGREDIENTS

serves 4–6

2.2 lb. – 1 kg SQUASH
COARSE SALT to taste
6 tablespoons EXTRA VIRGIN OLIVE OIL
SALT and PEPPER to taste
1 medium ONION
1 tablespoon RICE MALT, honey, or raw
cane sugar
5 tablespoons APPLE CIDER VINEGAR

EQUIPMENT

a saucepan
absorbent paper towels
transparent plastic wrap
a serving dish

Difficulty	**AVERAGE**
Preparation Time	**15 MIN. + 10 MIN.**
Cooking Time	**15 MIN.**
Method of cooking	**STOVETOP**
Microwave	**NO**
Freezing	**NO**
Keeping Time	**3 DAYS**

SPECIAL NOTE

Peddlers once commonly sold hot baked squash
that was eaten plain. The seeds, toasted and
sprinkled with salt, were a "treat," like
lupine seeds.

RECOMMENDED WINES
Oltrepò Pavese Pinot grigio (Lombardy):
dry white wine served at 50°F / 10°C
Montescudaio bianco (Tuscany): dry white wine served at 50°F / 10°C

❖

1 Clean the squash, remove the peel and the seeds and wash. C
into slices a little under a half inch – 1 centimeter thick, then
thinner slices. Place them on a plate and sprinkle with coarse salt. L
them sit for about 10 minutes, then dry with absorbent paper towel

2 Heat the oil in a saucepan, add the squash slices a few at a tim
and brown on both sides, turning with a slotted spatula. Remov
from the saucepan and drain on paper towels, add salt and pepp
and set aside.

3 In the same saucepan, place the peeled, washed and finely slice
onion, sprinkle with the rice malt and let it wilt without brownin;
stirring often with a wooden spoon. Then add the vinegar and
tablespoons water, and continue cooking over moderate hea
stirring occasionally, until the liquid has been reduced to half.

4 Place the slices of squash on the serving dish and drizzle with th
prepared dressing. Let them cool, then cover with transparent plasti
wrap and refrigerate several hours before serving.

PRACTICAL SUGGESTIONS
*For this recipe to be successful, you should only use very high qualit
squash. You can increase the amount of vinegar to a cup if you want
more flavorful dish.*

Cheese Torte

INGREDIENTS

serves 4

1/4 lb. — 100 g MASCARPONE (a rich Italian
cream cheese)
scant 1/4 lb. — 80 g GORGONZOLA
1/4 lb. — 100 g STRACCHINO (a mild, soft
Italian cheese)
4 WALNUTS
1 tablespoon WHOLE GREEN PEPPERCORNS

EQUIPMENT

a blender
4 molds

Difficulty	EASY
Preparation Time	10 MIN. + 3 HOURS
Cooking Time	NO
Method of cooking	NO
Microwave	NO
Freezing	NO
Keeping Time	2 DAYS

SPECIAL NOTE

Mascarpone is a specialty from Lombardy; it could
once be found at the dairy or butcher's shop,
packaged in gauze, in bundles weighing 1/4 or
1/2 lb. — 100 or 200 grams.

RECOMMENDED WINES
Dolcetto d'Acqui (Piedmont): light red wine served at 57°F / 14°C
Valtellina (Lombardy): light red wine served at 57°F / 14°C

1 Place the mascarpone, the gorgonzola, and the stracchino in the blender and whip for about two minutes, or until the cheeses are well–blended.

2 Break the nuts and remove the kernels. Place two in the blender with the green peppercorns and whip quickly one more time (the nuts and peppercorns should not be ground too finely).

3 Place the mixture into four small molds that you have moistened with a bit of water. Even out the surface and place them in the refrigerator 2–3 hours.

4 When ready to serve, remove the molds from the refrigerator, turn them out and decorate each torte with a half a walnut kernel.

PRACTICAL SUGGESTIONS

If you don't have green pepper, you can prepare these tasty tortes with a few pink or white peppercorns, or even a pinch of red pepper.

Cheese and Ham Paté

INGREDIENTS

serves 4

1/2 lb. – 200 g SMOKED HAM
1/4 lb. – 100 g ROMAN RICOTTA
1/2 lb. – 200 g MASCARPONE
a pinch of NUTMEG
half a small cup BRANDY
SALT and PEPPER to taste
a handful PINE NUTS
several WALNUT KERNELS

EQUIPMENT

a blender
a pâté mold
aluminum foil
a serving dish

Difficulty	**EASY**
Preparation Time	**15 MIN. + 3 HOURS**
Cooking Time	**NO**
Method of cooking	**NO**
Microwave	**NO**
Freezing	**NO**
Keeping Time	**2 DAYS**

SPECIAL NOTE

One hundred grams of smoked ham contain:
21.18 g protein, 36.42 g fats, 0.75 g
carbohydrates, 0.75 g vitamin B, 10 mg calcium,
166 mg phosphorous, 2.9 mg iron, and 421
calories.

RECOMMENDED WINES
Dolcetto d'Asti (Piedmont): light red wine served at 57°F / 14°C
Colli Perugia rosso (Umbria): light red wine served at 57°F / 14°C

1 Finely mince the ham, and place in the blender with the ricotta, mascarpone, nutmeg, brandy and a pinch of salt and freshly ground pepper. Blend for a few seconds, or until the mixture becomes smooth and creamy.

2 Line a pâté mold with aluminum foil and add the mixture. Smooth the surface, then refrigerate several hours.

3 When time to serve, immerse the mold in hot water for a few seconds. Turn out onto a serving dish, remove the aluminum foil and decorate with pine nuts and walnut kernels.

PRACTICAL SUGGESTIONS
This tasty dish is good for an elegant luncheon, and is excellent accompanied by whole wheat toast (perhaps cut into pretty rounds or star shapes). Toast them in the oven and, if you like the flavor, lightly rub them with a clove of garlic. Paté is the Italian spelling of the French pâté.

Hardboiled Eggs with Mushroom Sauce

RECOMMENDED WINES
Albana di Romagna secco (Emilia Romagna):
mellow, aromatic white wine served at 50°F / 10°C
Breganze bianco (Veneto): dry white wine served at 50°F / 10°C

Place a generous amount of salted water in a small skillet, bring to a boil and add the eggs. Let them boil for 8 to 10 minutes. Drain, un under cold water to stop the cooking, then peel and set aside.

In the meantime, soften the dry mushrooms in a bowl of lukewarm water and milk for about 30 minutes. Rinse, squeeze well and mince.

Place the cream in a small saucepan and heat with the broth over moderate heat. Add the mushrooms and minced parsley, a pinch of salt and freshly ground pepper, and mix with a wooden spoon, blending the ingredients well until you have a creamy mixture.

Slice the hardboiled eggs lengthwise and place on a serving dish. Pour the mixture over them and serve immediately.

INGREDIENTS
serves 6

4 EGGS
2 oz. – 50 g DRIED MUSHROOMS
1 scant cup CREAM
1/2 cup VEGETABLE BROTH
1 tablespoon minced PARSLEY
1/2 cup MILK
SALT and PEPPER to taste

EQUIPMENT
a bowl
a small saucepan
a small skillet
a serving dish

Difficulty	AVERAGE
Preparation Time	10 MIN. + 30 MIN.
Cooking Time	10 MIN.
Method of cooking	STOVETOP
Microwave	NO
Freezing	NO
Keeping Time	1 DAY

PRACTICAL SUGGESTIONS
To prevent the eggs from breaking while boiling, they should be at room temperature. You should thus take them out of the refrigerator at least 10 minutes before cooking. Rather than immersing them in boiling water as indicated in the recipe, you can immerse them in cold water and bring it to a boil. In this case, they will need to be boiled 5 or 6 minutes.

SPECIAL NOTE
For an egg to be tasty, the chicken must have the right kind of food. Problems with feed composition can result in eggs that taste like fish or hay.

Mediterranean Panini   p112

Rice Balls   p113

Celery Antipasti   p114

Stuffed Brussels Sprouts   p116

Spinach Puffs   p118

Eggs in Orange Sauce   p120

Pizza alla marinara   p122

All-Season Antipasti

Smothered Frittata Squares

INGREDIENTS

serves 4

1 ONION
1 clove GARLIC
4 tablespoons EXTRA VIRGIN OLIVE OIL
1 lb. – 400 g PLUM TOMATOES
SALT and PEPPER to taste
1 pinch OREGANO
6 EGGS
1 teaspoon WHITE FLOUR
2 tablespoons GRATED PARMESAN
50 G – 1 BUNCH BASIL
1 FRESH MOZZARELLA

EQUIPMENT

a skillet
a mixing bowl
a frying pan, a baking dish
absorbent paper towels

Difficulty	AVERAGE
Preparation Time	15 MIN.
Cooking Time	40 MIN.
Method of cooking	STOVETOP AND OVEN
Microwave	YES
Freezing	NO
Keeping Time	1 DAY

SPECIAL NOTE

In Italy, the terms *frittata* (omelet) and *pesce d'uovo* (a folded omelet) have been in use since the 15th century. The French term *omelette* is more recent.

RECOMMENDED WINES
Alto Adige Lagrein rosato (Alto Adige): rosé served at 54°F / 12°C
Regaleali rosato (Sicily): rosé served at 54°F / 12°C

1 Peel, wash and finely mince the onion and clove of garlic, place in a skillet with 2 tablespoons oil and brown gently. Then add the crushed plum tomatoes, and season with a pinch of salt and pepper and a dash of oregano. Let it reduce over moderate heat for about 20 minutes. Preheat the oven to 350°F.

2 Beat the eggs in a mixing bowl with a pinch of salt and pepper, add the flour, grated parmesan, and washed, dried and finely minced basil, and blend the mixture well. Place in a frying pan in which you have heated the remaining oil. Let the frittata harden on one side and then, using a slotted spatula or cover, turn it over and complete cooking on the other side. Place it on a paper towel to absorb excess oil, and cut into squares.

3 Arrange the frittata squares in a baking dish, pour the tomato sauce over them, sprinkle with grated mozzarella and bake until the cheese is completely melted. Serve immediately.

PRACTICAL SUGGESTIONS
If you cook the frittata in a cast iron skillet, remember that it shouldn't be washed, but cleaned with cornmeal mixed with salt, heated very hot and brushed with a cloth and then paper towels.

Crostini Primavera

Recommended Wines

Itrepò Pavese Pinot bianco (Lombardy): dry white wine served at 50°F / 10°C
Biferno bianco (Molise): dry white wine served at 50°F / 10°C

Thoroughly wash the arugula leaves, dry them well, mince finely
th the green beans (previously boiled for 10 minutes in a pan with a
all amount of boiled, salted water) and the ham.

Beat the ricotta to a cream in a mixing bowl, add the grated
rmesan, season it with a pinch of salt, then blend in the minced
ugula and beans and mix well with a wooden spoon. Now cut off the
ust from the slices of bread, brush each one with some melted butter
d bake at 350°F.

In the meantime, melt the remaining butter over a small double
iler, break the eggs into it, mix in 2 tablespoons milk, add a few
ops Worcestershire sauce, and season with a pinch of salt and
shly ground white pepper. Move the eggs quickly with a fork until
ey have become soft, scrambled and slightly hardened. Remove the
htly browned croutons from the oven, spread the minced
getables and then the eggs on top, place on a heated serving dish
d serve immediately.

Practical Suggestions

your prefer smaller crostini, perhaps to garnish other appetizers, you can
the slices of bread into triangles. You can also use slices of French bread
homemade bread.

INGREDIENTS
serves 4

a few leaves ARUGULA (GARDEN ROCKET)
1/3 lb. – 120 g FROZEN GREEN BEANS
1/4 lb. – 70 g HAM
1/2 lb. – 200 g RICOTTA
2 tablespoons GRATED PARMESAN
1/4 cup – 50 g BUTTER
SALT and PEPPER to taste
16 SQUARE SLICES BREAD
5 EGGS
2 tablespoons MILK
a few drops WORCESTERSHIRE SAUCE

EQUIPMENT
a pot
a mixing bowl
a small saucepan
a serving dish

Difficulty	**AVERAGE**
Preparation Time	**20 MIN.**
Cooking Time	**20 MIN.**
Method of cooking	**STOVETOP AND OVEN**
Microwave	**YES**
Freezing	**NO**
Keeping Time	**1 DAY**

SPECIAL NOTE
Some of the most important mineral salts in milk
are calcium and magnesium phosphates, which
strengthen bones during growth and
prevent rickets.

The Cardinal's Eggs

INGREDIENTS

serves 4

2 teaspoons VINEGAR, 4 EGGS
3/4 lb. – 300 g SMALL SHRIMP
1 tablespoon EXTRA VIRGIN OLIVE OIL
1 clove GARLIC, SALT and PEPPER to taste
1 tablespoon BÉCHAMEL SAUCE,
1/2 lb. – 200 g PÂTE BRISÉE PASTRY SHELLS
1/8 cup – 20 g BUTTER, 1 tablespoon WHITE
FLOUR

For the sauce

1 BLACK TRUFFLE, 2 oz. – 1 bunch each CHIVES,
PARSLEY, CHERVIL, 1 EGG, 2 EGG YOLKS, 1 pinch
SUGAR, 2 half eggshells OF WHITE WINE VINEGAR,
SALT, PEPPER and CAYENNE PEPPER to taste

For the garnishing

1 oz. – 20 g SALMON EGGS
8 slices TRUFFLE

EQUIPMENT

3 saucepans, a bowl, a blender

Difficulty	ELABORATE
Preparation Time	40 MIN.
Cooking Time	45 MIN.
Method of cooking	STOVETOP AND OVEN
Microwave	YES
Freezing	NO
Keeping Time	1 DAY

SPECIAL NOTE

Eggs should not be washed before you put them
in the refrigerator, to avoid removing the natural
protective coating that prevents air and odors
from penetrating them.

RECOMMENDED WINES
Collio Tokay from Friuli (Friuli Venezia Giulia): mellow aromatic white
wine served at 50°F / 10°C
Bolgheri rosato (Tuscany): rosé served at 54°F / 12°C
❖

1 In a saucepan, boil the water with the vinegar. Break the eggs int
a dish and let them slide one by one into the boiling water. Cook fc
about 3 minutes. Remove with a slotted spoon, place on a cloth an
trim the edges.

2 Clean the shrimp (setting aside 4 for the sauce) and chop int
pieces. Place them in a saucepan with the oil and unpeeled garli
add salt and pepper, and sauté for 2 minutes. Drain into a bow
remove the garlic, and cool. Then add the béchamel, blend it and se
it aside.

3 Prepare the sauce. Whip the remaining shrimp, scrub the truffl
and mince it. Also mince the chives, parsley and chervil. Place
whole egg and 2 egg yolks in a small saucepan with the sugar, mix
bit, add 2 half eggshells of water and 2 of vinegar, the salt, peppe
and cayenne. Place the saucepan in a double boiler over the heat an
whip the mixture until it has doubled in volume and become dense
without boiling.

4 Remove from the heat, add the truffle, the minced herbs an
whipped shrimp, and mix well. Spread the shrimp and béchame
mixture on the bottom of the pastry shells, place the poached egg
on top and the prepared sauce over it. End by placing the salmo
eggs and sliced truffle on top. Place the pastries on a baking shee
and bake at 350° for a few minutes. Serve hot or lukewarm.

PRACTICAL SUGGESTIONS
These egg tarts are so rich that they're fit for a Cardinal. You can even ser
them an as entrée without a first-course. Just increase the ingredients.

Crêpe Torte

INGREDIENTS

serves 6

3/4 lb. – 300 g CARROTS,
4 EGGS
1 head CHICORY (or endive)
15 prepared CRÊPES
MAYONNAISE to taste
various COLD CUTS (prosciutto, ham, coppa, tongue, etc.)
CHICKEN SALAD as necessary

EQUIPMENT

2 bowls
a small saucepan
a serving dish

Difficulty	EASY
Preparation Time	20 MIN.
Cooking Time	10 MIN.
Method of cooking	STOVETOP
Microwave	NO
Freezing	NO
Keeping Time	2 DAYS

SPECIAL NOTE

The French word *crêpe* is internationally used to indicate very thin, either savory or sweet pancakes that become crispy during cooking.

RECOMMENDED WINES
Grignolino del Monferrato casalese (Piedmont):
light red wine served at 57°F / 14°C
Chianti classico (Tuscany): medium-bodied red wine served at 61°F / 16°

1 Clean and trim the carrots, wash them and chop into thin strip and place in a bowl. Wash the chicory and chop it thinly, then plac in another bowl and set aside.

2 Place a generous amount of salted water in a small saucepa bring it to a boil and add the eggs. Let them cook 8 to 10 minute Drain, run under cold water to stop the cooking, then peel them, cu them into rounds and set aside.

3 Spread a layer of mayonnaise on the first crêpe, then add one the ingredients indicated (cold cuts, chicory, chicken salad, a fe rounds of hard–boiled egg, etc.).

4 Place the second crêpe on top, spread with mayonnaise, add th filling, and go on to the third crêpe, and so on, until you hav finished the ingredients and the cake has reached a sufficient heigh

5 The last crêpe, which acts like a cover, should be spread wit mayonnaise on the inside, and the outside should be decorated wit dollops of mayonnaise. Serve the crêpe torte on a serving dish.

PRACTICAL SUGGESTIONS
This torte can be served not only as antipasti (or appetizer), but also as cold single-dish meal, perfect for lunch. The ingredients in the layers can as varied as your imagination.

Avocado and Shrimp Salad

INGREDIENTS

serves 4

2 medium AVOCADOS
I lb. – 400 g SHRIMP
I/2 lb. – 200 g CANNED PALM HEARTS
I head of LETTUCE
SALT and PEPPER to taste
For the Sauce
half a LEMON
I EGG
4.5 TABLESPOONS EXTRA VIRGIN OLIVE OIL
I tablespoon WHISKEY
SALT and WHITE PEPPERCORNS to taste
I tablespoon RED COCKTAIL SAUCE

EQUIPMENT

a steam cooker
a mixing bowl
a small bowl
a bowl

Difficulty	AVERAGE
Preparation Time	30 MIN.
Cooking Time	2 MIN.
Method of cooking	STOVETOP
Microwave	NO
Freezing	NO
Keeping Time	I DAY

SPECIAL NOTE

Palm hearts are the pith of the stems of palm
leaves, processed industrially and commonly sold
boiled and canned.

RECOMMENDED WINES

Alto Adige Pinot bianco (Alto Adige): dry white wine served at 50°F / 10°
Ischia bianco (Campania): dry white wine served at 50°F / 10°C

1 Wash the avocado, cut it in half and remove the seed. Using
spoon, remove the pulp and cut into cubes, and set aside the tw
empty skins. Shell the shrimp and wash in cold water, drain and dr
Steam cook for 2 minutes, drain and set aside. Drain the palm hear
and cut into rounds. Trim the lettuce, select 8 small leaves, wash, d
and place in the avocado skins. Cut the remaining lettuce into strip
wash, drain and dry. In a mixing bowl, mix the prepared avocado pu
with the shrimp, the strips of lettuce, the palm hearts and a pinch
salt and pepper.

2 Prepare the sauce. Squeeze the lemon and put the juice in a sma
bowl. In another bowl, put a pinch of salt and a few drops of lemo
Add the egg yolk and mix with a wooden spoon or a whip. Drop b
drop, pour in a little of the oil, mixing clockwise constantly. Whe
the sauce begins to thicken, add the remaining oil in a thin strean
alternating with a few drops of lemon juice if it becomes too thic
When the oil is absorbed, season the sauce with the salt, fresh
ground pepper and remaining lemon juice. Add the whiskey and re
sauce and mix. Season the prepared salad with a tablespoon of sauc
mix it gently and distribute in serving cups. Serve accompanied b
the remaining sauce.

PRACTICAL SUGGESTIONS

Once you have opened the can of palm hearts, remove any remaining hear
immediately. You can store them in the refrigerator for a couple of days in
covered glass container.

94

Bresaola, Mozzarella and Grapefruit

INGREDIENTS

serves 4

1/4 lb. – 100 g finely chopped BRESAOLA
(dried salt beef)
I LEMON
2 tablespoons EXTRA VIRGIN OLIVE OIL
SALT and PEPPER to taste
I fresh COW BUFFALO MOZZARELLA
I GRAPEFRUIT

EQUIPMENT

a small bowl
transparent plastic wrap
an oval serving dish

Difficulty	**EASY**
Preparation Time	**15 MIN. + 24 HOURS**
Cooking Time	**NO**
Method of cooking	**NO**
Microwave	**NO**
Freezing	**NO**
Keeping Time	**I DAY**

SPECIAL NOTE

Bresaola is a typical cold cut from Valtellina, and
is prepared with the best cuts of tender young
or adult beef, salted and dried.

Recommended Wines
Valtellina Superiore Inferno (Lombardy): full–bodied red wine
served at 61°F / 16°C
Grignolino d'Asti (Piedmont): light red wine served at 57°F / 14°C

I Arrange the bresaola on an oval serving dish. Dissolve the juic
of half a lemon in a small bowl with a tablespoon olive oil, add sal
and freshly ground pepper, and season the slices of bresaola with thi
mixture. Cover the plate with transparent plastic wrap, an
refrigerate

2 Shortly before serving, cut the mozzarella into broad, thin slice
and set aside. Peel the grapefruit, remove the white part and cut int
thin slices.

3 Remove the bresaola from the refrigerator, and place th
mozzarella and grapefruit slices on top, alternating in two rows. Sal
pepper and season with the remaining lemon juice and oil, an
garnish with fresh parsley if you like. Serve.

Practical Suggestions
*This is an original variation of bresaola and grapefruit Gritti, which doe
not call for mozzarella. As this is a refined dish, pay special attention t
presentation.*

Cucumber–Peanut Salad

INGREDIENTS

serves 4

1 bunch WHITE CELERY
1 CUCUMBER
3/4 lb. – 300 g SCAMORZA CHEESE
4 tablespoons ROASTED PEANUTS
4 tablespoons EXTRA VIRGIN OLIVE OIL
1 tablespoon MUSTARD
SALT and PEPPER to taste

EQUIPMENT

a mixing bowl
a small bowl
a blender

Difficulty	EASY
Preparation Time	15 MIN.
Cooking Time	NO
Method of cooking	NO
Microwave	NO
Freezing	NO
Keeping Time	1 DAY

SPECIAL NOTE

The peanut is a leguminous plant that is a native of Brazil and was imported to Africa by the Portuguese. Its seeds are highly nutritious.

RECOMMENDED WINES
Biferno bianco (Molise): dry white wine served at 50°F / 10°C
Breganze bianco (Veneto): dry white wine served at 50°F / 10°C

1 Wash and clean the celery, peel the cucumber and slice very thinly, then place the slices in a mixing bowl. Cut the scamorza into small thin slices, then add them to the celery and cucumber.

2 Place the peanuts into the blender (setting a few aside for garnishing), grind them finely and sprinkle over the prepared celery and cucumber.

3 Using a wooden spoon, dissolve the oil with the mustard in a small bowl, mixing to obtain a uniform dressing for the prepared salad. Salt, pepper and carefully mix. Garnish with the peanuts you set aside and serve.

PRACTICAL SUGGESTIONS
If you like, you can use almonds, hazelnuts, walnuts or pistachios instead of peanuts. If you want to enhance the somewhat exotic flavor of this appetizer, serve it with bananas sliced lengthwise and dotted with butter.

Crêpe Rolls in Gelatin

INGREDIENTS

serves 6

2 EGGS
scant 1 cup — 120 g WHITE FLOUR
SALT to taste
1 1/2 cups MILK
OLIVE OIL to taste
1/2 lb. — 200 g CANNED HAM PÂTÉ
1/3 lb. — 120 g SALMON sliced thinly
2 cups — half a liter PREPARED GELATIN
1 tablespoon LEMON JUICE

EQUIPMENT

a bowl
a cast iron frying pan
a skillet
a serving dish

Difficulty	**AVERAGE**
Preparation Time	**30 MIN. + 3 HOURS**
Cooking Time	**30 MIN.**
Method of cooking	**STOVETOP**
Microwave	**NO**
Freezing	**NO**
Keeping Time	**3 DAYS**

SPECIAL NOTE

The most commonly known pâté is made of liver, while pork pâté was popular in ancient Rome, the Middle Ages and Renaissance times.

RECOMMENDED WINES

Blanc de Morgex (Valle d'Aosta): dry white wine served at 50°F / 10°C
Isonzo Tokay del Friuli (Friuli Venezia Giulia): mellow, aromatic white wine served at 50°F / 10°C

1 Beat the eggs in a bowl with the flour and a pinch of salt, then dilute everything with the milk until you have a uniform mixture. Pour the batter a little at a time into a hot, lightly oiled frying pan to form crepes as thin as possible.

2 Spread a little ham pâté on one crêpe, place a second crêpe on top and make a layer of salmon. Continue, alternating ingredients until they are finished. Roll this up into a compact cylinder and refrigerate for about an hour.

3 Remove the roll from the refrigerator, slice it and arrange it attractively on a serving dish.

4 Melt the prepared gelatin in a skillet, add the lemon juice and pour everything over the rolled crepes. Refrigerate at least 2 hours before serving.

PRACTICAL SUGGESTIONS

You can decorate this dish by pouring more liquid gelatin on a tray until you have a layer a little less than a quarter inch — half a centimeter thick. When it has completely solidified, cut it with special crescent, star or disk–shaped molds and place them all around the plate.

Whole–Wheat Mini–Pizzas with Spinach

RECOMMENDED WINES

Oltrepò Pavese Cortese (Lombardy): mellow, aromatic white wine served at 50°F / 10°C

Colli Martani Grechetto (Umbria): dry white wine served at 50°F / 10°C

❖

1 Clean the spinach well, wash it repeatedly in abundant running water and cook in a pot in only the water remaining after washing and briefly draining. When done, drain, squeeze, mince finely and season in a saucepan with 2 tablespoons oil, salt and freshly ground pepper. Cut the mozzarella into cubes.

2 Preheat the oven to 350°F. Mound the flour on a cutting board, pour 4 tablespoons oil on it, and knead it with enough water to make a smooth, elastic dough. Roll out, and using a glass, cut out little pizzas that are not too thick. Arrange on a lightly oiled baking sheet.

3 Spread a small quantity of plum tomatoes on the pizzas, along with a teaspoon spinach, one or two cubes of mozzarella, salt and pepper, a few drops oil and the oregano. Bake in a preheated oven for 10–15 minutes and serve.

PRACTICAL SUGGESTIONS

Don't throw away the spinach cooking water, which is rich in mineral salts. You can use it to prepare a tasty soup, for example with rice and potatoes. These mini–pizzas are also excellent prepared with chard rather than spinach.

INGREDIENTS
serves 4

2 lb. – 800 g SPINACH
8 tablespoons EXTRA VIRGIN OLIVE OIL
SALT and PEPPER to taste
5 cups — 500 g WHOLE–WHEAT FLOUR
1/2 lb.– 200 g CANNED PLUM TOMATOES
1 FRESH MOZZARELLA
1 tablespoon OREGANO

EQUIPMENT
a saucepan
a pot
a baking sheet

Difficulty	AVERAGE
Preparation Time	20 MIN.
Cooking Time	30 MIN.
Method of cooking	STOVETOP AND OVEN
Microwave	YES
Freezing	YES
Keeping Time	2 DAYS

SPECIAL NOTE
Spinach is best before it has begun flowering. After it flowers, the leaves grow tougher, fibrous and harsh–tasting.

Beef Morsels

INGREDIENTS

serves 4

I APPLE
about 1/2 lb. – 250 g GROUND BEEF
I EGG
SALT and PEPPER to taste
2 LEMONS
I SCALLION
WHITE FLOUR as necessary
PEANUT OIL for frying
2 HARDBOILED EGGS
2 oz. – I bunch PARSLEY

EQUIPMENT

a mixing bowl, a saucepan for fried food
a metal spatula, an egg–slicer, a tray
a few wooden skewers
absorbent paper towels

Difficulty	AVERAGE
Preparation Time	45 MIN.
Cooking Time	20 MIN.
Method of cooking	STOVETOP
Microwave	NO
Freezing	NO
Keeping Time	I DAY

SPECIAL NOTE

Lemons were sacred in the Islamic world and
served as talismans. In fact, it was said that the
devil could never enter a house where there
were fresh lemons.

RECOMMENDED WINES
Rubino di Cantavenna (Piedmont): light red wine served at 57°F / 14°C
Pomino rosso (Tuscany): light red wine served at 61°F / 16°C

1 Peel and finely grate the apple. Put it in a mixing bowl with th
ground beef, the egg, the salt, the pepper, a tiny bit of grated lemo
zest and the peeled, washed and finely minced scallion. With the ai
of a wooden spoon, mix everything well and make small, perfectl
round little meatballs about the size of large cherries. Carefull
smooth them with your hands, flour them and place them on a fla
surface.

2 When they are all prepared, heat the oil in a saucepan until it i
quite hot, and add 8–10 meatballs at a time. Let them cook, the
remove from the saucepan with a metal spatula and place o
absorbent paper towels for a moment. When the meatballs are al
fried, slice the hardboiled eggs with the egg–slicer, and using a shar
knife, also cut the lemons in their skins very thinly.

3 Place the sliced lemons on the bottom of a tray, place a piece o
sliced egg on each one and put a meatball in the center of it. Skewe
the ingredients vertically along with a sprig of parsley, which will ac
as a garnish. Serve.

PRACTICAL SUGGESTIONS
*A good kitchen rule says you should only use frying oil one time. T
remove the odor of fried food from the kitchen, burn an orange peel or
sugar cube over the gas burner.*

Golden Potato Crostini

INGREDIENTS

serves 4

1 lb. — 400 g POTATOES
3 tablespoons GRATED CARROTS
SALT to taste
1 1/2 tablespoons CORNMEAL
1 EGG WHITE
12 slices HOMEMADE BREAD
1 tablespoon SESAME seeds
3 tablespoons PARSLEY
PEANUT OIL for frying

For garnishing
2 BELL PEPPERS, cut into strips

EQUIPMENT
a pot, a potato ricer, a mixing bowl
a cast iron frying pan, a serving dish
absorbent paper towels

Difficulty	AVERAGE
Preparation Time	30 MIN.
Cooking Time	30 MIN.
Method of cooking	STOVETOP
Microwave	YES
Freezing	NO
Keeping Time	1 DAY

SPECIAL NOTE
Crostini, here in the form of a large slice of homemade bread, either fried or toasted, are of ancient origin. In the Middle Ages, they took the place of an individual dish, soaked in sauce.

RECOMMENDED WINES
Frascati (Lazio): dry white wine served at 50°F / 10°C
San Severo rosato (Puglia): rosé served at 54°F / 12°C

1 Wash and thoroughly scrub the potatoes, and boil them in a pot of salted water. Peel and rice, and place the mixture in a large mixing bowl. Add the grated carrots, adjust the salt, add the cornmeal and the egg white. Blend everything well and spread the mixture on the slices of bread.

2 Separately mix the sesame seeds with the minced parsley, and use this mixture to sprinkle the slices of bread. Lightly press the mixture so it adheres well.

3 In a frying pan, preferably of cast iron, heat a generous amount of oil, then add the croutons, being sure that the oil covers them completely. Brown them uniformly on both sides, remove with a slotted spatula and place on absorbent paper towels to remove any excess oil.

4 Arrange on a serving dish garnished with green peppers cut into slices, and serve hot.

PRACTICAL SUGGESTIONS
You can accompany these savory crostini with French mustard or ketchup, as you prefer. The serving dish should be decorated with thin strips of red and yellow bell peppers.

Spinach Salad with Ricotta and Avocado

INGREDIENTS

serves 4

1 lb. — 500 g SPINACH
1 AVOCADO
1/2 lb. — 200 g RICOTTA
4 tablespoons EXTRA VIRGIN OLIVE OIL
2 tablespoons LEMON JUICE
SALT and PEPPER to taste

EQUIPMENT

a blender
a serving dish

Difficulty	EASY
Preparation Time	20 MIN.
Cooking Time	NO
Method of cooking	NO
Microwave	NO
Freezing	NO
Keeping Time	1 DAY

SPECIAL NOTE

The avocado is a fruit that is not sweet and very fatty. In fact, it has 240 calories for every 1/4 lb. — 100 g of edible portion. The most common hybrid is the Fuerte variety. The fruit is green, and it is cultivated in the Mediterranean.

RECOMMENDED WINES
Trentino Riesling Renano (Trentino): dry white wine served at 50°F / 10°C
Alcamo (Sicily): dry white wine served at 50°F / 10°C

1 Trim the spinach, eliminating any spoiled leaves, then wash carefully a number of times under running water, dry very gently and chop coarsely.

2 Cut the avocado in half, remove the seed, and use a teaspoon to remove the pulp. Place it in the blender and add the ricotta, oil, and lemon juice, season with a pinch of salt and a bit of freshly ground pepper.

3 Blend for a few moments until you have a smooth, uniform dressing for the spinach. Mix again thoroughly and serve.

PRACTICAL SUGGESTIONS
This original, cool appetizer is especially pleasant in the summer. However, you must have small, tender spinach. You can use 1.5 oz. — 30 grams walnuts, almonds or pine nuts instead of avocado.

Mozzarella Rounds

INGREDIENTS

serves 4

2 FRESH MOZZARELLAS
1/2 lb. – 200 g BLACK OLIVES
a few leaves BASIL
2 tablespoons EXTRA VIRGIN OLIVE OIL
1 teaspoons OREGANO
SALT and PEPPER to taste
1 small CUCUMBER

EQUIPMENT

a small bowl
a chopping knife
a serving dish

Difficulty	EASY
Preparation Time	15 MIN.
Cooking Time	NO
Method of cooking	NO
Microwave	NO
Freezing	NO
Keeping Time	1 DAY

SPECIAL NOTE

Until a few decades ago, cottage industry mozzarella was produced only in a few areas of central–southern Italy, especially in the lowlands of Lazio, Campania and Puglia.

RECOMMENDED WINES
Trebbiano di Romagna (Emilia Romagna): dry white wine served at 50°F / 10°C
Cerveteri bianco (Lazio): dry white wine served at 50°F / 10°C

1 Cut the mozzarellas into 8 rather thick slices and arrange on serving dish. Pit the olives, and using a chopping knife, mince ther finely with the washed, dried basil (setting a few leaves aside for th final garnishing).

2 Put the oil, the previously prepared minced mixture, the oregano and the salt and freshly ground pepper into a small bowl and blend everything together with a wooden spoon. Spread this cream on the slices of mozzarella and refrigerate.

3 Shortly before serving, peel the cucumber and cut into thin slices Remove the mozzarella from the refrigerator, and decorate the surface with the slices of prepared cucumber and a few basil leaves. Serve immediately.

PRACTICAL SUGGESTIONS
If you're in a hurry, you can buy ready–made olive paste and spread it on the sliced mozzarella. Then sprinkle it with oregano and a few chopped basil leaves.

Vegetable Calzoni

INGREDIENTS

serves 4

2.2 lb. – 1 kg ENDIVE
PITTED BLACK OLIVES to taste
POWDERED RED PEPPER to taste
SALT to taste
EXTRA VIRGIN OLIVE OIL to taste
a scant 1 lb. – 350 g RISEN BREAD DOUGH
1 tablespoon WHITE FLOUR

EQUIPMENT

a mixing bowl
a rolling pin
a baking sheet

Difficulty	AVERAGE
Preparation Time	30 MIN.
Cooking Time	30 MIN.
Method of cooking	OVEN
Microwave	YES
Freezing	YES
Keeping Time	2 DAYS

SPECIAL NOTE

Calzone is a sort of savory pizza pocket typical of southern Italy. It consists of yeasted or short pastry filled in various ways, folded into a crescent shape and baked or fried.

RECOMMENDED WINES
Cirò bianco (Calabria): dry white wine served at 50°F / 10°C
Freisa di Chieri secco (Piedmont): light red wine served at 54°F / 12°C

1 Trim, wash and drain the endive well, gather into bunches an chop into thin strips. Place it in a mixing bowl with the pitte olives, the red pepper, and a pinch of salt. Season everything with tablespoons extra virgin olive oil and let it rest. Preheat the oven 450°F.

2 In the meantime, divide the bread dough into 4–6 parts, and usi a rolling pin, roll out onto a lightly floured board. Pull them gent until they are oval in shape.

3 Oil the baking sheet, arrange the oval pasta forms, spread portion of the prepared mixture on each one, and fold back the past to seal the edges. Lightly oil the surface of the calzoni, bake them f about 30 minutes and serve hot.

PRACTICAL SUGGESTIONS
To prepare these calzoni, you can use chard or spinach instead of endive. you like, you can also use black pepper and a pinch of nutmeg instead of r pepper, and add a few pieces of anchovies in oil.

Mediterranean Panini

INGREDIENTS

serves 4

half a GREEN OR YELLOW BELL PEPPER
half A RED BELL PEPPER
2 tablespoons EXTRA VIRGIN OLIVE OIL
I ONION
2 HARDBOILED EGGS
4 ANCHOVY FILLETS IN OIL
12 PITTED BLACK OLIVES
SALT and PEPPER to taste
4 soft, ROUND ROLLS

EQUIPMENT

a frying pan
a serving dish

Difficulty	EASY
Preparation Time	15 MIN.
Cooking Time	5 MIN.
Method of cooking	STOVETOP
Microwave	NO
Freezing	NO
Keeping Time	I DAY

SPECIAL NOTE

The ancient Greeks learned the art of yeasted bread and oven baking from the Egyptians. In Athens during the time of Pericles, there were as many as 72 different types of bread.

Recommended Wines
Valdadige bianco (Trentino): dry white wine served at 50°F / 10°C
Ostuni bianco (Puglia): dry white wine served at 50°F / 10°C

I Wash the peppers, remove the seeds and internal white parts, cu into strips and sauté in oil for a few minutes in a frying pan.

2 Peel, wash and finely mince the onion, cut the rolls in half an remove the soft inner portion.

3 Then place slices of hardboiled egg, a few pepper strips, a bit of rav minced onion, a fillet of anchovy, a few black olives and a pinch of sa and freshly ground pepper on each of the four lower half rolls. Cove them with the upper half, arrange on a serving dish and serve.

Practical Suggestions
Before filling the sandwiches, you can spread them with a little butter. I you want the peppers to be more flavorful, sprinkle them with a bit of finel minced basil. To save time, you can use canned peppers cut into wide strips drain them well and add a few drops of olive oil.

Rice Balls with Lemon

RECOMMENDED WINES

Ruché di Castagnole Monferrato (Piedmont): light red wine
served at 57°F / 14°C
Trebbiano di Romagna (Emilia Romagna): dry white wine
served at 50°F / 10°C

Place a generous amount of water in a pot. When it comes to a boil, salt it and cook the rice al dente, then drain and cool.

Place the oil, lemon juice, salt, freshly ground pepper, washed and minced parsley and garlic and one grated lemon zest into a bowl, and using a fork, blend all ingredients well.

Season the rice with the resulting sauce, add the grated parmesan, mix well and use this mixture to make numerous walnut–sized balls.

Cut the remaining lemons into thin slices and arrange them harmoniously on a serving dish. Place a rice ball on each lemon slice and decorate with a caper. Place several sprigs of parsley on the edge of the plate and serve.

PRACTICAL SUGGESTIONS

To prevent the rice from becoming gummy as it cooks, don't mix it. You can also add a tablespoon olive oil to the cooking water (which will also prevent the water from bubbling out of the pot), If you want a whiter rice, add a few drops of lemon juice to the cooking water.

INGREDIENTS

serves 4

2 cups — 250 g RICE
4 LEMONS
5 heaping tablespoons — 100 g GRATED PARMESAN
1 clove GARLIC (optional)
1 sprig PARSLEY
1 teaspoon CAPERS IN VINEGAR
4 tablespoons EXTRA VIRGIN OLIVE OIL
SALT and PEPPER to taste

EQUIPMENT

a pot
a bowl
a serving dis

Difficulty	AVERAGE
Preparation Time	15 MIN.
Cooking Time	15–18 MIN.
Method of cooking	STOVETOP
Microwave	NO
Freezing	NO
Keeping Time	2 DAYS

SPECIAL NOTE

Like all citrus fruits, lemons are of Oriental origin. The name comes from the Arabic *laimum* and the Persian *limun*, which refer to citrus fruits in general.

Celery Antipasti

INGREDIENTS

serves 4

1 bunch CELERY
5 oz. – 150 g STRACCHINO CHEESE
SALT and PEPPER to taste or paprika
1 tablespoon GRAPPA
1 tablespoon GRATED PARMESAN

EQUIPMENT

a bowl
a pastry bag
a serving dish
ta

Difficulty	**AVERAGE**
Preparation Time	**20 MIN. + 1 HOUR**
Cooking Time	**NO**
Method of cooking	**NO**
Microwave	**NO**
Freezing	**NO**
Keeping Time	**1 DAY**

SPECIAL NOTE

It is said that during his old age, Molière ate primarily parmesan cheese, which he knew was full of energy–rich substances and easily digestible.

RECOMMENDED WINES
Cortese di Gavi (Piedmont): mellow, aromatic white wine served at 50°F / 10°C
Cirò bianco (Calabria): dry white wine served at 50°F / 10°C

1 Wash and dry the celery, cut it at the base and remove all the stalks. Discard the outer stalks and select the best ones. Cut them into pieces of equal length (about 6 inches – 13 centimeters), setting aside a few leaves for garnishing. Line these pieces up carefully on a serving dish.

2 Place the stracchino in a bowl, add the grated cheese, a pinch of salt and freshly ground pepper, and using a wooden spoon, work it until it becomes a very uniform cream. Add the grappa, mix again and place the prepared cream in a pastry bag and refrigerate for at least an hour.

3 When it is time to serve, remove the cream from the refrigerator and fill the celery. Decorate the serving dish with the celery leaves you set aside, and serve.

PRACTICAL SUGGESTIONS
These delicious celery boats are just as good if you use other soft cheeses instead of the stracchino, such as gorgonzola (not too aged), roquefort or robiola.

Stuffed Brussels Sprouts

INGREDIENTS

serves 4

1 1/2 lb. – 600 g BRUSSELS SPROUTS
can be frozen

1 tablespoon WHITE WINE VINEGAR
or apple cider vinegar

2 oz. – 1 bunch FINE HERBS (tarragon,
parsley, chervil, chives)

SALT and PEPPER to taste

3 tablespoons CREAM

1/4 cup – 40 g BUTTER

1 RED BELL PEPPER, cleaned

EQUIPMENT

a corer

a small saucepan

a saucepan

a small pan

a serving dish

Difficulty	**AVERAGE**
Preparation Time	**20 MIN.**
Cooking Time	**40 MIN.**
Method of cooking	**STOVETOP**
Microwave	**NO**
Freezing	**NO**
Keeping Time	**2 DAYS**

SPECIAL NOTE

Chervil (Anthriscus cerefolium), a native of the
Middle East and southern Russia, was brought to
the West by the Romans. It is used quite often in
French cuisine.

Recommended Wines
Prosecco di Conegliano (Veneto): mellow, aromatic white wine
served at 46°F / 8°C
Orvieto classico (Umbria): mellow, aromatic white wine served at 50°F / 10°C

1 Clean the Brussels sprouts, wash and dry them, and cut a cros
form into the base. Bring a generous amount of water to boil in a pot
salt it and add the vinegar and bunch of herbs, and cook the Brussels
sprouts for six minutes. Drain, chop one third of them coarsely, anc
using a corer, remove the central portion of the remaining sprouts anc
chop this as well. Sieve both the chopped sprouts and the centra
portion of the hollowed sprouts and place into a small saucepan.

2 Place over the heat and cook, stirring constantly with a wooder
spoon. Season the mixture with salt and pepper and continue
cooking, stirring constantly and letting it reduce. Finally, add the
cream and half the butter in pieces, mix and set aside. Clean and wash
the pepper and chop into cubes.

3 Place the hollowed Brussels sprouts in a saucepan with the
remaining butter and sauté several minutes. Salt and pepper, and add
a few tablespoons water. Cover and continue cooking for about 10
minutes over moderate heat. Remove from the heat, widen the
hollow in the middle and fill with the previously prepared puree
Garnish by placing a cube of pepper in the center and serve on a
serving dish.

Practical Suggestions
For this recipe to be successful, the Brussels sprouts must be cooked al dente.
To fill them, you can use a pastry syringe with a fluted tip for a guaranteed
aesthetic effect.

Spinach, Pea and Mushroom Puffs

INGREDIENTS

serves 4

1/8 cup – 35 g BUTTER,
1 heaping 1/4 cup – 35 g WHITE FLOUR,
6 tablespoons – 2 dl MILK, SALT to taste
12 PUFF PASTRIES (prepared with choux pastry),
For the fillings
spinach filling: 1/2 lb. – 200 g SPINACH
1 oz. – 20 g BUTTER, 4 tablespoons GRATED
PARMESAN, 12 small slices SMOKED HAM
pea filling: 1/2 LB. – 200 G PEAS,
1/8 cup – 25 g BUTTER,
4 tablespoons GRATED PARMESAN, NUTMEG to
taste, 12 small slices LARD
mushroom filling:
F1.5 oz. – 30 g DRIED MUSHROOMS,
1 oz. – 20 g BUTTER,
4 tablespoons GRATED PARMESAN,
12 sliced MUSHROOMS

EQUIPMENT

a skillet, a mixing bowl, a pot

Difficulty	**AVERAGE**
Preparation Time	**30 MIN.**
Cooking Time	**45 MIN. – 1 HOUR**
Method of cooking	**STOVETOP AND OVEN**
Microwave	**YES**
Freezing	**NO**
Keeping Time	**2 DAYS**

SPECIAL NOTE

Spinach, originally from the Caucasus and Persia,
was introduced to Europe between the 9th and
15th centuries. The wild variety *(Chenipodium
bonus–henricus),* known as Good King Henry,
is also excellent.

RECOMMENDED WINES

Dolcetto di Dogliani (Piedmont): light red wine served at 57°F / 14°C
Valpolicella della Valpantena (Veneto): light red wine served at 57°F / 14°C

1 Prepare the béchamel by frying the butter with the milk, flour
and a pinch of salt for 15 minutes. Preheat the oven to 350°F.

2 Boil the spinach in a pot, squeeze it, place in a mixing bowl and
season with the butter and grated parmesan. Blend the mixture with
the béchamel and then, using a pastry syringe, fill the puffs, and then
cover with a thin slice of smoked ham. Place on a baking sheet and
bake 15 minutes.

3 If you prefer peas to spinach, boil them, put them through a
vegetable mill and season with butter, parmesan and nutmeg. Mix
with the béchamel and proceed as for the spinach filling. The only
variation is using a slice of lard to wrap the puff.

4 A third alternative is mushroom filling. Soften, squeeze and finely
mince the mushrooms, mix with the butter and parmesan and mix
with the béchamel. Before putting the puffs in the oven, cover with
the sliced mushrooms.

PRACTICAL SUGGESTIONS

*If you have many guests, you can serve these delicious puffs by tripling the
ingredients for the béchamel sauce and making 12 pastries with spinach, 12
with peas and 12 with mushrooms.*

Eggs in Orange Sauce

INGREDIENTS

serves 4

6 EGGS
8 oz. – 200 g MAYONNAISE
1 ORANGE
1 squirt KETCHUP
1 squirt WORCESTERSHIRE SAUCE
POWDERED RED PEPPER to taste
CREAM as necessary
SALT to taste

EQUIPMENT

a skillet
a serving dish
a bowl

Difficulty	**EASY**
Preparation Time	**15 MIN.**
Cooking Time	**10 MIN.**
Method of cooking	**STOVETOP**
Microwave	**NO**
Freezing	**NO**
Keeping Time	**1 DAY**

SPECIAL NOTE

Around 1808, a French gourmet catalogued 543 recipes using eggs. Today, experts tell us that there are thousands of codified eggs recipes.

RECOMMENDED WINES

Albana di Romagna secco (Emilia Romagna): mellow, aromatic white wine served at 50°F / 10°C
Verdicchio di Matelica (Marche): dry white wine served at 50°F / 10°C

1 Boil a generous amount of salted water in a skillet. Immerse the eggs (which should be at room temperature) and bring them to a boil over moderate heat. After 5 minutes, drain them, run under cold water to stop the cooking and let them cool to lukewarm. Peel them, cut them in half and place on a serving dish.

2 Place the mayonnaise, juice of half an orange, the ketchup, the Worcestershire sauce and a pinch of red pepper in a bowl, mix with a wooden spoon and, a little at a time, add enough cream to make a rather thin sauce. Adjust with a pinch of salt and pour over the eggs.

3 Cut the remaining orange into slices, place on the serving dish around the eggs and garnish with fresh parsley. Serve.

PRACTICAL SUGGESTIONS

You can prepare an orange sauce without using mayonnaise, by substituting it with an equal amount of ricotta. Mix with the ingredients indicated and blend with a wooden spoon to make it very creamy and uniform.

Pizza alla marinara

INGREDIENTS

serves 4

1/2 lb. – 250 g PLUM TOMATOES

3 leaves BASIL

2 cloves GARLIC

3 ANCHOVY FILLETS IN OIL

WHITE FLOUR as necessary

3/4 lb. – 300 g YEASTED BREAD DOUGH

pinch of OREGANO

SALT as necessary

EXTRA VIRGIN OLIVE OIL as necessary

EQUIPMENT

a rolling pin

a round baking pan

Difficulty	EASY
Preparation Time	10 MIN.
Cooking Time	20 MIN.
Method of cooking	OVEN
Microwave	YES
Freezing	YES
Keeping Time	2 DAYS

SPECIAL NOTE

Anchovies are clupeid fish that live their total existence in enormous, so–called "polarized" schools that in practice act as a single "superindividual."

RECOMMENDED WINES
Capri bianco (Campania): dry white wine served at 50°F / 10°C
Riviera Ligure di Ponente Pigato (Liguria): dry white wine served at 50°F / 10°C

1 Preheat the oven to a very hot 480°F. Prepare the tomatoes, wash and dry them, remove the skin and seeds and slice. Wash, dry and chop the basil, and mince the garlic and anchovies as well.

2 Place a bit of flour on the cutting board and roll out the dough into a round, disk shape. Place this in the oiled pizza pan.

3 Arrange the tomato slices on the dough in the pan, leaving about a one inch border. Add the minced garlic and anchovies. Sprinkle the surface with oregano, the chopped basil, and a pinch of salt. Drizzle with a bit of oil and bake for 15–20 minutes, or until sizzling. Serve immediately.

PRACTICAL SUGGESTIONS
This typical dish from Campania is as nutritious as a first course. If you like, before cooking you can add capers or pitted black olives to the pizza.